PRINTED IN THE UNITED STATES OF AMERICA

B&P

To

MARY

and

Diane
Laura
Richard
Kathy
Edward
Maryann

Acknowledgment

To all whose immeasurable contributions helped to make this book possible, some of whom appear in the text, and to:

Mr. Don Benson,

For rigid training that helped me to fully understand the true meaning of the axiom, "There are two sides to every question";

Mrs. William J. Donald,

For original notes and papers on management by her late husband;

Mr. Fred D. Lehn,

For career counseling, warm friendship, and encouragement;

Mr. I. Mande,

For his unselfish cooperation in providing me with many case histories;

Mr. Leslie D. Price,

My confidant during formative years who received a young engineer as a fellow professional;

Mr. E. H. Wipperman,

For notes on executive performance and for his personal interest and encouragement over a decade;

Mr. Joseph F. Miller,

For free rein to perform my job as I thought best, and for NEMA's financial assistance in graduate work at Columbia and Syracuse Universities and for other self-development aids, including the Dale Carnegie courses which gave me the self-confidence needed to write a book.

What This Book
Will Do for You

There are two kinds of people—
The Doers and the Onlookers. The book was written on the
premise that most people would rather be the first kind—if they
only knew how. Most experienced executives make good decisions.
A few, like Mr. W. H. Satterfield of Steel City Division, Midland
Ross Corporation, seem to know instinctively the right thing to do
and the right way to do it. It is not easy to compete with such
individuals and with those who are better educated, more person-
able, and more technically qualified. The truly ambitious can, however, develop the necessary executive arts and skills to even the
score, and cross over the often narrow line between success and
failure.

A new breed of employee challenges the old school of management, and it takes a new kind of executive skill to direct the
modern worker who is smarter, better educated, but also more independent and harder to manage than his predecessor.

In a series of ten lessons you will be *shown how* to custom fit
your self-development program to your individual needs, how to
establish realistic goals, and how to make leadership attributes an
integral part of *your* personality.

Specific know-how is provided in the form of such practical direction as: Five ways to Greater Efficiency; Four Golden Keys to problem solving; Four home rules for more conference skill; Ten Cures
for Conference blues; Eight Hints for preparing a successful task;
Twelve Confidence Boosters for speaking up on all occasions; How
to organize yourself; How to play it straight with executive know-
how; the strategy of subtle discipline; the knack of compatible
(hence more effective) supervision; how to develop personal re-

11

sponsibility and delegate it to others; how to handle the seven most common disciplinary problems; a success formula for non-direct counseling—when and how to use direct counseling; how to "see through" employee gripes; the three how's of turning liabilities into assets; how to make your "handicaps" work *for* you; how to say it better; "inside" tips on developing a winning writing style by arousing interest, informing and persuading your readers; and much more.

What this book can do for *you* depends heavily upon your own inner strength of purpose and perseverance. Develop the right success attitude and YOU can master executive arts and skills.

Contents

13

Mastering

Executive Arts

and Skills

CHAPTER ONE

Design a Self-Development
Course to Suit YOU

You can develop executive know-how. It is not too late; you are not too old.

Executive know-how is not a supernatural ability granted to only a fortunate few. Inherited traits and environment, though important, merely dictate how much personal effort you must expend to develop executive know-how.

You are not born with executive ability as such; you are born with a certain potential; that is, inherited physical or mental attributes that make it easier or harder for you to develop the necessary executive know-how.

Last winter a fire raged through a tenement, injuring many and killing some. Four small children survived because of the bravery of a thirteen-year-old boy. Not once, but four times this incredible youngster entered the burning building and led each of the small children to safety, because they were his cousins and he "could do no less." The hero of that day, though only thirteen years old, kept his head when others about him were panicking. That boy has executive potential.

Only time will show what this youth makes of his leadership attributes, because *ability is not the same as performance.* Executive performance is the implementation of executive know-how.

No amount of training materially alters inherited potential, but it can be buried at a very early age or developed, depending upon environmental conditions, inertia, the lack of ambition, and educa-

19

tion. "Average" achievement may conceal either great executive potential or below-average talent. Through persevering effort a less gifted, but more ambitious individual can climb the management ladder, while the "genius" may trail behind.

The larger reserve of executive talent lies on a continuum between those who lack executive traits and those who are amply blessed with leadership potential. Most business leaders have abilities which lie somewhere between the two extremes.

By no means, however, are you competing with *all* members of the "reserves." Many are disqualified because of such handicaps as age, poor health, lack of essential training, insufficient drive or motivation, or bad habits. That leaves plenty of room at the top for *you*, so don't become an executive dropout through failure to develop the know-how which can open new vistas of success for you.

Achievement is tied to *action;* use all your resources to advance and stay ahead of those who will not try as hard. Be ready for that opportunity when it comes.

During a losing streak of a major league baseball team, a desperate call for help went out to the farm team. The ace pitcher on the farm had literally pitched himself into complete exhaustion, so the "second best" was sent up—and became a star player. Fate often plays a dominant role, but sometimes it can be countermanded—if you are prepared. Always try to be ready for the job you want.

Give yourself a better chance for executive success by custom-designing a development program to suit *you:*

1. Establish realistic goals.
2. Determine how much you are willing to pay for success.
3. Make the most of your innate and developed abilities.
4. Program your course.
5. Measure your progress.

Establish Realistic Goals

Reaching for the moon is fine for astronauts. Everything points to their making it, but I am not making any plans to go there in the foreseeable future. The most attainable goal is the most realistic one.

Realistic goals take into account your known limitations as well as the forces that will be helping or impeding your progress. You are much more likely to reach your goal if you know:

Who You Are
Where You Are Now
How You Will Get There

WHO ARE YOU?

I know a young fellow who wanted to be a sales executive. Married while still in school, he was, upon graduation from college, already the father of an infant boy. He could not afford to wait for exactly the right opening. Consequently, after a few fruitless tries at his desired objective, he reluctantly settled for what was immediately available—a professorship in a small rural school. Dragging his feet and feeling sorry for himself, he embarked upon his "distasteful" occupation.

Within a very short time, his wife told me, the young man was attending his students' sports events, rooting and encouraging them to victory, and sympathizing with their losses. The last I heard of him, he had enrolled at his local university to take additional courses in education and school administration.

I predict a brilliant and rewarding career for this lucky young man who discovered early in the game who he really was.

Approximately seventy-five percent of those who obtain executive posts either lose them or yield them to others. Some of those who drop out of management redirect their energies to the professions or private enterprises, and they are more successful or content! Some executive dropouts choose to take manual, clerical or other "unexecutive" roles and are happier!

Many of these dropouts had the executive know-how to perform adequately, but some sold their ambitions short. Others had no real concept of their abilities or limitations; they did not know who they were. Not knowing who you are can make you a miscast, playing the wrong part all your life.

Things were not going well for Jim Tyler, the new office supervisor. Jim blamed it on his surly subordinate, Charley Sloan, whose sneering attitude bordered on the very brink of insubordination. Tyler could not bring himself to reprimand Sloan, because Sloan gave his young superior an inferiority complex. Tyler's sense of inadequacy was further aggravated by Sloan's obvious status with his co-workers.

Worrying about how he was going to get rid of Sloan, Tyler never saw that Sloan's disrespect for him was actually the outspoken expression of *all* his subordinates' contempt for his inability to command the proper respect for his position and his person.

Now several years later Tyler is trying to get up the next rung of the executive ladder, but his lack of executive know-how is holding him back. It will continue to hold him back because he does not know that he lacks executive know-how. He is waiting for the "big day" when he will leap over those who, because of luck, passed him on the way up.

Every personality problem is not the other fellow's personality. Essential to successful self-development is the ability to see yourself as you really are. This requires that you recognize your shortcomings along with your merits. Don't kid yourself.

Be Realistic. We are all self-loving creatures who try to evade those facts unflattering to ourselves; consequently wishful fancy often obscures the true picture of a situation. We tend to look on the bright side of ourselves. For example, if you are passed over in a promotion, before you blame anyone, probe *your own* performance and personality traits for the reason.

There is a general hypothesis that personality predicates performance, with ability to get along with people considered to be indicative of success. The personal characteristics of those who make it to the top as well as of those who don't make the grade seem to bear out this theory, but neither this hypothesis nor the subsequent theory can be accepted as absolute. Personal characteristics are only one of several major factors at work in executive advancement; namely, personality traits, relationship with the executive(s) who make the selection, luck, timing, etc.

Large vs. Small Companies

Executive counselors generally agree that the larger the company, the more opportunity for advancement, and the greater the fringe benefits. There is, however, a very important "but"—unless you get a real "charge" out of strong competition, you may get lost in the shuffle. Or, if being known by your first name matters strongly to you, you will probably be happier and do better in the small company.

The location of your place of employment can also be important if you are either the big city or hometown type. Also, your progress can depend upon how long it takes you to get to and from work. Unless you are completely sold on the merits of suburban vs. city living, long hours of commuting can get you down and seriously reduce the quality and quantity of your output.

To be the head of a mouse or the tail of an elephant is a decision that you can make intelligently only if you know who you really are!

What Should Your Role Be? If you have doubts about what your role should be, seek constructive criticism and increase your worth accordingly. Since advice is easy to give and hard to take, make it a little easier for you to follow wise counsel by enlisting the aid of impersonal advisors. Take advantage of scientific testing to help you discover who you are and what you can do!

The two basic requirements for a scientific test are:

1. Reliability—It will produce the same results each time.
2. Validity—It measures the characteristics indicated. For instance, if a test is designed to rate aptitude it should not report attitudes.

Psychological Tests. These tests pertain to the science of the mind. They can help you to choose a career for which you are intellectually and emotionally suitable. This is advantageous because it will be difficult, if not impossible, for you to yield the desired performance if you are miscast.

In studying engineering, for example, the misfit but persevering student often can earn his degree, but if he has to concentrate all his energies on making passing grades in the required subjects, he will be unable to apply this knowledge to mining, construction, etc. Thus his chances of success in engineering are poor.

Intelligence Tests. These tests measure the mental capacity for a certain position. General intelligence is the innate ability which has been most thoroughly explored in the field of psychological research, because it is so essential for performance in most occupations.

It is not, however, the only factor to be considered when selecting your career or field of operation, because equal capacity for learning under equal conditions does not always yield the same performance. Early experiences, drive, and perseverance produce in each person different incentives to learn and advance.

Your test score on intelligence tests is compared with that of other individuals in similar groups. Consequently, intelligence quotients (I.Q.) are tests based upon norms which have been established for the nation as a whole.

Achievement Tests. These tests have one major drawback; they can measure the abilities of those who are experienced, but cannot forecast how a novice will perform in any particular field. Nor is it possible to predetermine how quickly you will progress on the job. The only true measure of achievement is performance on the job, which is generally impracticable before employment.

The general achievement tests cover educational background and are designed primarily to measure occupational proficiency. As might be expected, such tests are more readily adaptable to skilled and semi-skilled workers, but they can be developed for junior executives—if tailored to specific needs.

Aptitude Tests. These tests are designed to measure those individual characteristics considered to be most indicative of your capacity to acquire a specific knowledge or ability with training. These tests endeavor to correlate certain personal traits to the achievement of others possessing similar characteristics. Fairly reliable estimates of probability have resulted therefrom.

How Much Is Your Goal Worth?

Lazy people are likely to fail as executives. Managerial obligations are time consuming and demand the expenditure of a great amount of energy. Constant application of enthusiastic effort is needed to reach any significant goal and stay there. If it sometimes seems that the bold and the brave are favored by circumstances, it is because they are!

It takes courage and determination to throw off mediocrity and the shackles that restrain and divert your attention from your long-range goals. You will falter at the crossroads and unmarked detours. Be prepared for despondency, apprehension and distracting objectives to constantly court your favor. You may have to temporarily neglect your family and sacrifice some of your leisure time.

What is your objective worth to *you* in terms of effort and time required to get where you want to go?

One executive who "made it" began the long hard pull when he was a very small boy growing up on a Georgia farm. Generations of apathy and shiftlessness had reduced this lad's once proud family to "poor white."

From somewhere long back in his heritage came an awakening, a growing dissatisfaction with things as they were. His earliest recollections are of his family's low status in a town that was named for one of his ancestors. Step by step, he fought his way out of his socioeconomic class. He worked and saved to put himself through college and graduate school of an ivy league university.

Today he and his children occupy a social and economic position far removed from that man's beginning. One of the prices he paid for success was the erection of an unbridgeable gap between himself and his old family ties.

Believe it or not, this man's remarkable achievements broke his father's heart!

WHERE ARE YOU NOW?

If you are currently employed, you probably prefer to advance within your present organizational structure. In that case, what are your chances for promotion? Take an instant to see exactly where you stand in your company. If an organizational chart doesn't exist, make your own totem pole of your company's structure. Be sure that it goes from the top down to the lowest echelon (*Figure 1*).

The next step is to size up your competition. Your major competitors are your peers (not your boss)! What advantages do they have over you, or you over them? What are their handicaps? Examine their backgrounds for work experience, education, special talents, seniority, relationship with management. How do your qualifications compare with theirs?

If, for instance, you are the only one without a college degree, much younger than the next oldest one, and less able to communicate or to take on more responsibility, you have a long road to travel before you realize your objective. On the other hand,

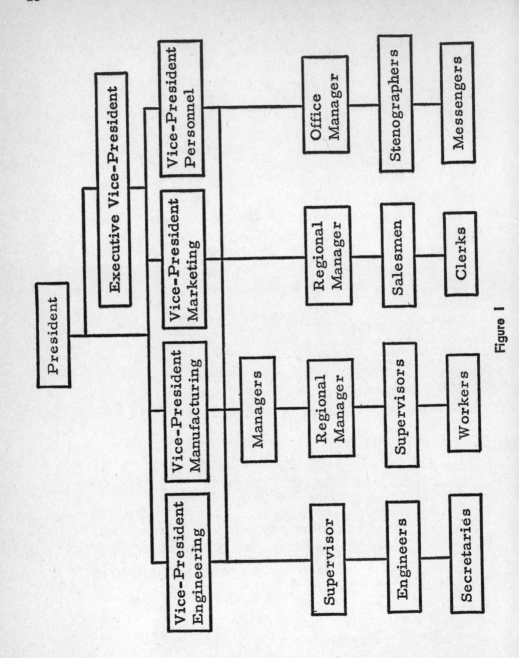

Figure 1

maybe just a little more executive know-how is all you need to swing the odds in your favor.

If you must migrate in order to advance, never go empty handed. Always take something of value with you—like more executive know-how. Start *now* to narrow the gap between where you are and where you want to be.

How Will You Get There?

Now that you know *who* you are and what you can do, specifically define your short and long range goals.

Make the Most of Your Abilities

It is very important to have realistic intermediate objectives. Don't exaggerate your potential contributions and expect to start at the top! A development program tailored to fit your individual needs will help you to avoid the hit-or-miss approach that can leave you with no more significant know-how than you now have.

Plan to:

> *Add to your job knowledge*
> *Master executive techniques*
> *Get in the spotlight*
> *Substitute good habits for bad ones*

Believe that you can develop executive know-how as others before you have done under similar conditions and *swing into action!*

Marshal every available resource at your disposal to develop the necessary executive know-how to make you more valuable to your employer and to society. Take advantage of every opportunity to progress that comes your way.

Add to Your Job Knowledge

If you are still in school or under 30, specialization may be your "open sesame" to success. There is an accelerating demand for experts in every field. The results of your aptitude and intelligence tests may point the way for you.

Usually, the smaller companies cannot afford the luxury of specialists. If you choose to cast your lot with a small outfit, expect to perform more than one function. The more you know how to do, the more valuable you are in the eyes of a small business owner.

Certainly consider:

1. How will specialization help me in advancing in my chosen field?
2. Is there likely to be an opening in my company to utilize the specialized skill or knowledge?
3. Is the course or training sanctioned by my employer?
4. Is specialization an escape from failure to perform adequately in my present job?
5. Will skills now possessed complement those required in my ultimate goal?

Get all the information you can on the area that interests you. Go to the library, visit schools, talk to those already in that field. Many courses can be taken on a non-degree basis.

Formal vs. Do-It-Yourself Training

There are pros and cons to self-study and formal classroom education. As a general rule, the advantages of courses at an accredited school outweigh a do-it-yourself program through a library or a correspondence course, but your self-improvement program consistently followed can advance you further than the one who indifferently or apathetically undergoes formal schooling. Nevertheless, if you can do well on your own initiative you would probably do even better with the assistance of a college education.

Don't forget that the primary objective of your self-development is eventual executive performance rather than the mere accumulation of knowledge. *Keep your eyes on the goal.*

Know Your Company Inside Out

1. What are the goals and objectives of your firm?
2. Learn whether or not the overall policies are being followed, and how they are being altered at different places in the organization.
3. Study the organization which has been established to obtain the desired objectives of the company.
4. Learn the resources available to your firm.
5. Analyze the plant layout, the equipment, materials handling, worker performance, attitude and employee morale.

6. Review the specific and general operations of each unit (marketing, production, distribution, etc.), learning its problems and advantages over other segments of the organization.
7. Keep in constant sight the purposes of the business.
8. Understand the interdependence between associates, departments, companies, industries, government, and the general public.

Don't concentrate too hard on any one phase, or try to learn every little detail of each operation performed by others. Stand back far enough from the daily monotony to see the overall workings of the organization and the relationship of each operation.

Increase your worth through:

Libraries	Executive organizations
Special outside courses	Executive conferences
Company courses	Training by superiors
Lectures	Publications and periodicals

Group Conferences. These are practical for learning *en masse,* and relatively inexpensive when compared to individual instruction. You will find most training conferences held during hours when you will be most alert; they are usually limited to one to one and a half hours and generally scheduled on a regular basis.

In a training course you are the one being taught, but do not withhold comments which you believe will contribute profitably to the discussion. You make the best suggestions when you have mastered the technique of "like to like" and "kind to kind."

A dentist friend of mine is a skilled user of this technique, and he is richer for it. Like all dentists, Fred maintains a complete file on all of his patients; he goes one step further than most, however, by taking before and after photographs. These pictures are not just reference data, they are Fred's best "sales agents," because Fred is smart enough to show a 40-year-old prospect the before and after picture of a 30-year-old satisfied client. Fred is also too smart to "over-do" his sales pitch by trying to fool an elderly patient into thinking she can look like a 20-year-old "after treatment."

Assume for the moment that your company produces heavy

electrical mining machines, and that it has the know-how and essential facilities to expand into other fields such as electric cars, diesel locomotives, etc. Ask yourself, "Has any other company made a similar successful transition? Will the personnel fit into the resulting new environments, particularly in dealing with new clients?"

When you participate in a conference or discuss the plans of the company with others having management responsibility in the firm, "time in" on what you hear—not what you want or think they should say.

If the discussion is about the future plans of the company, you will remember better and gain insight into the proposed course of action, if:

1. You *see* the profit picture of present operations and the potential in other fields, short and long range, including fluctuations in the business cycles.
2. You *grasp* the predisposition of your management (conservative or liberal by either age or personality).
3. You *identify* the elements of your company as they would relate to new environments. (Salesmen who regularly call on mine superintendents might feel ill at ease if they must confront the chief purchasing officers of such firms as the Penn-Central Rail System in competition with salesmen from a company like General Motors Corporation which provides substantial freight for railroads.)
4. You *understand* the economic resources of your firm to produce a more acceptable product, and create any needed status image.

Participate as much as possible in the work of committees for excellent training in conference know-how and ability to speak up with confidence!

Don't shortchange yourself by failing to take advantage of *all* such opportunities to develop executive know-how.

It is a common practice to select for advancement by the superior's observation of the worker's performance on the job. You will be given specific assignments, and the manner in which you perform will be indicative of your developed proficiency, so look for opportunities to accept responsibilities. Jump at any chance to make decisions in line with your capabilities.

Master Executive Techniques

You demonstrate executive know-how when you:

Have the right Executive Look.
Learn the knack of Compatible Supervision.
Use Positive Discipline for better results.
Get more out of your subordinates through Counseling.
Speak up with Confidence.
Give your writing Sales Appeal.
Are not afraid to Make Decisions.
Turn liabilities into Assets.
Thrive in any Organizational Climate.

The above techniques and more are clearly outlined in this book.

Get in the Spotlight

Your advancement depends largely upon superiors noting with favor your work performance.

Ned Hutchinson was getting nowhere in his organization, and it was giving him ulcers. His doctor recommended an outside interest—anything that would get his mind off his company and its frustrations. Ned joined his local association of Young Republicans and threw himself wholeheartedly into its activities. In less than a year, he was one of the organizers. Soon his fund-raising efforts became so successful that the local newspapers lauded Hutchinson for his achievements.

But even before Ned's fame spread through the community, his superiors had already begun to sit up and take note of the "new," self-confident Ned Hutchinson. He is now vice-president in charge of public relations!

Is there a group in your organization (or outside) in which you can "shine"? Look around for ready-made areas in which to practice your budding executive know-how! It may be a church group, the YMCA, professional societies, the country club, political organizations, community activities, conferences, trade associations, chamber of commerce, special courses—to mention but a few.

Don't immediately "take over" a group. Listen and watch attentively the various personalities at work. Observe especially the characteristics of those in charge Volunteer for those assignments not desired by the established members of the group. Work hard and seek the advice and guidance of the older members, and before you know it, you are on the "inside" and ready to take on more sophisticated responsibilities.

When you shine in one or more outside activities, let this information flow back to your company management. Active participation and leadership in community affairs will most assuredly result in more executive know-how, along with much personal satisfaction. These benefits cannot help but carry over into your work environment, and are the surest methods of inoffensively getting in the spotlight of management's quest for executive talent.

Constructive work off the job, while your associates are taking it easy, will not arouse the same resentment that would emanate from over-zealous performance on the job. Your co-workers will not feel that your behavior is casting aspersions on their work habits. Activities outside the office are not viewed as unfair competition, so get out there and really "shine" in those "non-competitive" areas.

Substitute Good Habits for Bad Ones

"How do I this habit break? As you did that habit make." Repetition is the basis of all training.

It is easier to form new habits than to erase old ones, the stronger of which tend to recur under stress.

Enumerate those traits that you desire but lack, and those that interfere with achievement. Even though you are intelligent and possess a broad base of knowledge, you may be missing some important qualities that can hold you back.

Some authorities contend that performance—the true measure of an executive—is the true "brand" of leadership, rather than "executive traits." Nevertheless, personality controls the ability to perform in the human relations area of business, with the necessary physical and mental make-ups required for acceptable performance varying from job to job, company to company, and industry to industry. Adequate performance in one position may not be right for another—even the one immediately above it. You cannot, therefore, logically assume that you will automatically flow to the top on the basis of your present performance.

Your effort to improve your personality traits as they relate to executive know-how will not be materially affected by education whether learned in schools, libraries, or special courses. Proficiency in these areas must come on the job and here it is much harder to set time limits.

Development of executive personality traits should be directed toward the accomplishment of the following intermediate objectives:

1. Getting along with people on the job.
2. Staying healthy.
3. Thinking straight.
4. Making effective decisions.
5. Performing under tension.
6. Building self-confidence.
7. Remembering names, faces, places, dates, etc.
8. Profiting from mistakes (your own as well as those of others).
9. Communicating effectively.

The development of executive know-how requires that you learn to:

1. Organize yourself.
2. Be alert to the new avenues of better ways to proceed.
3. Influence others.
4. Demonstrate enthusiasm.
5. Think positively.
6. Build and maintain morale, through friendliness, praise, appreciation and understanding.
7. Accept and delegate responsibility.
8. Be flexible.
9. Plan and program.
10. Think on your feet.
11. Analyze and solve real problems.
12. Process ideas of others.
13. Obtain cooperation.
14. Avoid controversies.

With these broad objectives in mind, set out to develop one good habit at a time until it is part of your make-up, then move on to the next one. Since the modification or development of some traits takes more time than others, your time schedule must be flexible.

On the other hand, the development of some executive traits will demand little personal effort and time, allowing you to proceed rapidly to the development of the next one. You will find that the tempo of progress increases, because many executive characteristics complement each other.

For example, as you strive to inspire confidence in others, you will better understand them; this in turn requires objectivity and forthrightness. The development of self-control begets dignity. Problem solving is akin to ability to make decisions, and so forth.

Suit the rules to your individual capacity, but certainly take advantage of company courses, lectures, and conferences wherever available.

Schedule Your Program

Time is a necessary element in achieving proficiency at any task. Don't sit around daydreaming about what you are going to do "tomorrow." Every day do something, however small, toward your goal.

Once you have established the procedure that you will follow to get the necessary background education, set time limits for accomplishment, and stick to your schedule. Use the hours for schools, program of courses, conferences, etc., to help you make a realistic time schedule.

Your schedule should take into account whether you are pursuing limited, specific, or long-range objectives. The program aspects should cover the principal steps involved in the procedure and the time sequence in specific detail. The major variables in details are closely correlated with futurity—the more distant your goals, the more variables must be taken into consideration.

Do more in the same time by learning to read faster. Here are a few quick tips to help *you* read faster and better.

Recognize the Writing Pattern. You can read personal experiences much faster than technical data or other informative material. Pace yourself accordingly.

Skim. This is harder than at first appears. It takes practice to skim and absorb at the same time. If you are a word by word (or worse yet, a syllable by syllable) reader, start taking in a phrase at a glance, then a sentence, until you can take in most of a paragraph in one look. Teach yourself to remember without backtracking.

Don't be discouraged if you cannot learn to skim a whole page at a time. That may or may not come with practice. The important thing is that with practice, you will read faster and learn more.

Measure Your Progress

Your progress in developing executive know-how can be measured in terms of motivation, intelligence, and developed ability. This should be reflected in your increasing willingness to assume personal responsibility and a growing capacity to supervise the efforts of others.

Regularly evaluate your executive know-how in terms of how you influence others rather than trying to sum up your own productive efforts.

Grade your progress in achieving your intermediate goals as set forth on page 33. There must be no permanent knee on your learning curve. Progress is a continuing affair, consequently, as you study the personal characteristics which affect your executive performance, keep in mind that the gauge you have available is constantly changing.

Have an alternate plan of action to fall back on, or to use as a corrective measure, so that you do not drop out of your self-development program from failure to make the desired progress.

Drive or motivation is the common multiplier of your progress. Without this mysterious force, success is not possible. Executive performance can be expressed in terms of the following mathematical formula:

Executive performance $= D(W + O + R + K)$
Where:

$D =$ Drive or Motivation

$W =$ Wisdom (I.Q.—Intelligence quotient, acumen or intellect)

$O =$ Opportunities Utilized to Develop Executive Ability (Developed ability)

$R =$ Responsibility (Readiness to accept responsibility for your own actions as well as those of your subordinates)

$K =$ King or Master of Others (Supervisory ability)

By substituting the correct values in the foregoing equation, a reliable yardstick is available for determining the executive ability of a given person. Since the assignment of completely accurate factors is not possible, the formula is not perfect across the board. It can, however, be adapted for your use as a reasonable guide for most work environments.

Achievement is the result of the way you put your capabilities to work, and it is that factor by which you will most often be measured. Your professional actions should, therefore, be the end goal of the accumulation of executive know-how.

Review

Just as a business without direction or dynamics will stagnate, you too cannot progress by drifting aimlessly, depending upon luck or the will of the moment to guide you. Much like the race between the tortoise and the hare, those with less innate ability than others can often win out by continuing to press forward while their more gifted but lazy contemporaries procrastinate along the way.

The most successful self-development program is the one that is suited to the individual. This assures the establishment of realistic goals in terms of ability and cost in time, family relations, fatigue and financial outlay.

Your background, however notable, is seldom a passkey to assured success. The important thing is to *progress steadily toward your long-range goal.* Unless you establish definite guidelines, you cannot accurately measure your progress.

The ability to grow should be one of your outstanding traits. Knowledge can be increased by reading financial papers, business publications and good books on varying topics—preferably those of an informative nature. Supply your brain with the proper food for growth.

Make allowances for your natural reluctance to change, and include in your self-development plan:

1. Clearly defined goals.
2. Integrated and meaningful actions.
3. Adequate and scheduled time for the program.
4. The aid to be received from others.
5. Controls to avoid mistakes by anticipating difficulties.

6. The constant use of executive techniques—at home, in the office and in your social environment.
7. Objectivity in measuring your progress or self-analysis.

A complete development program includes special emphasis in some area disassociated with your job, but of interest to you. It matters little whether it's painting, building models, bird watching, gardening, etc., but whatever your choice, you should try to excel in it. The self-confidence alone derived from doing anything well is worth the effort.

CHAPTER TWO

Put On the Right
Executive Look

"Do not judge by appearances" is just about the best advice you will ever get. Heed it, if you can! The trouble is that most people do judge by appearances. The best executive know-how ideally presupposes a telescopic vision that penetrates outer coverings to reveal the naked truth, but knowing that *you are being judged by appearances* as well as by performance is also executive know-how.

At the starting line of the executive race you are literally "on your own" without the powerful support of past successful experiences which will fuel you later on. At this crucial initiation period, how you "come across" to others can either be a headstart for you or a handicap.

Last summer I had a luncheon date with an old school friend who is now a recruiting counselor for an executive employment agency. I waited for him in the outer office with a half-dozen or so young men from about 25 to 30 years of age.

All were well groomed! Some were tall; nearly all were at least medium height; one was handsome enough to have been a movie star; another wore glasses and read his magazine. All were presentable; all had come in response to this ad:

> TECHNICAL ASS'T
> TO PRESIDENT
>
> Financially sound small firm undergoing rapid expansion needs an engineer with 2–5 years in electro-mechanical or electronics design, development, test, production, or liaison experience. Engineering degree or equivalent experience necessary. Relocation at company expense. Starting salary $11–$13,500 + bonus and profit sharing. Our employees know of this ad.
>
> *Box 68673*

Of these applicants two were found to be more qualified than the others, but the serious looking young man in the dark-rimmed eyeglasses was given the first crack at the job over his best-dressed competitor. This piqued my curiosity, and I had to ask my friend, "Why?"

"My choice looked more the type that company would hire," I was told. "You know—intellectual, serious, dedicated. Did you notice what he was reading?" He mentioned a well known technical publication.

I found out later that the "intellectual" did get the job and that his good-looking contender is now thriving as a sales engineer where his appearance and M.E. Degree make exactly the right winning combination for *that* occupation.

APPEARANCES DO COUNT

Sometimes a candidate for a job is watched by hidden cameras, one-way vision walls, etc. as he is interviewed. How would you look? Except by self-imposition, there is no *one* "executive look" of race, creed or color, but there *does* seem to be some correlation between socioeconomic status, size, height, age and executive performance. This could be because executives as a whole are more socially acceptable, eat and dress better than other groups, or that companies prefer tall candidates as more impressive, less obvious in their ambitions, etc.

In any case, the popular "executive look" today seems to be young, healthy, lean and "hungry" (hungry meaning a searching, unsatisfied yearning, or "itch" for better things, as much as the physical attribute of slenderness). Everybody counts calories these days and the best looking clothes are obviously designed for the tall and thin, but there is more to the "executive look" than physical attributes and the "right clothes," important though they are.

With sufficient executive know-how, a fat, short fellow in baggy trousers sometimes makes it up the executive ladder, although it is harder for him to make the right first impression.

You are always going to find every type at the top—those who like people, hate people, are well educated, self-made, tall, short, fat, thin, etc. They are up there because the required executive performance varies with the geography, type and scope of each operation, as well as each company's "personality" which, like people, can be conservative, liberal, democratic, static, dynamic, unorthodox, etc.

Within the very same company, executive know-how calls for different abilities and personality traits to yield the desired performance.

The "right executive look" for a *Sales Manager* would project the optimism, enthusiasm, communication skill or "charm" that makes sales. Says Mr. Rudman of the Klein Institute for Aptitude Testing, "If you are hiring a salesman, you don't want him to be 6'6" and weigh 310 pounds, or he will overpower the client!"

A *Comptroller* (in addition to training and background) is, ideally, an accurate, detail conscious, somewhat skeptical no-nonsense type.

For a *Research Director* the "right look" is knowledgeable, conservative, dedicated. If in addition to that, the would-be researcher can also successfully convey to others his willingness to forego an immediate gain for the more worthwhile but distant achievement, he is almost sure to have the advantage over a candidate who wants to know, "What's in it for me *now*?"

So there *is* a definite link between success and the way you look, but there is also much more to success than the "right look"! I am thinking about the woman who wrote into the maker of a headache remedy: "I just love your ads, especially the TV commercials, and I hate to say it, but I buy —— (a rival product) because it works better."

You can look great, but if you can't do the job, you are likely to be on your way out. The right look is a big help, but desirable performance is the ultimate test of executive know-how.

A good way to put on the "right executive look" is to:

Follow the Leader

When in Rome do as the Romans do! To develop executive know-how, do as the executives do. This is a new version of the old children's game "Follow the Leader," but with the same old risk: You can get into trouble if you follow the wrong leader or don't recognize the right cutoff point.

Morton Wessler played "follow the leader" literally, but without executive know-how. So faithfully did Morton copy his superior that when he talked he sounded "just like the boss." That was the trouble. Morton only "sounded like an executive" to the management which overlooked his numerous other abilities.

The approach adapted by Morton flattered his boss, but when a successor to his superior was named, Morton was passed over. A carbon copy usually looks exactly like what it is.

Be a winner in the game of "Follow the Leader" by picking the right leader. Ask yourself:

What Is an Executive?

First of all, as the name implies, an executive is a *doer*. He causes things to happen, preferably good things, but sometimes bad—Adolf Hitlers and Al Capones also lead.

A successful executive exists in terms of what he does in each situation; he has a compulsion to strike through to new solutions; ideally, he is genuinely interested in people, and he has executive know-how.

At every opportunity, practice the basic techniques of successful executives in and out of your work area.

Executive attributes are those personal traits which are believed to be related to effective performance. To evaluate the executive know-how of the leader (or leaders) you wish to follow, be sure to consider the type of work and the organizational climate in which they operate. It makes a difference!

Grade your leader on the following attributes most generally regarded as executive traits.

Adaptability	Forcefulness
Ambition	Initiative
Appearance	Integrity
Approachability	Intelligence
Communicating Ability	Interests
Cooperation	Judgment
Courage	Moderation
Creativeness	Open-mindedness
Decision-Making Ability	Organizing Ability
Dependability	Perseverance
Energy	Responsibility
Enthusiasm	Self-confidence
Experience	Self-control

Sincerity
Social Awareness
Subordinates' Response

The leader you choose to follow should score high on all counts, because the omission of any needed characteristic for effective performance can be significant.

You look most like an executive when you:

Think Like an Executive
Act Like an Executive

Think Like an Executive

You think like an executive when you act on facts, not opinions.

Mr. H. H. Watson, consultant for several electrical companies recalls that the late manager of Association Services for Westinghouse Electric Corporation, Frank Thornton, Jr., never took what you said at face value. If Frank suggested to you, "Let's go out to dinner," and you turned out your empty pocket saying, "I can't afford it," Frank would say, "What about your other pockets?" If you still said, "No money there either!" Frank would come back at you with, "Do you want me to lend you some?"

This probing would continue until Frank was certain of your real reason for not joining him. There wasn't much you could keep from Frank Thornton, as many found out.

How Do You Think?

Pretend this morning you went back to sleep after the alarm clock sounded. Consequently you are later than usual starting out for work. If you make all your transportation connections without a single hitch you can still be at your desk on time. But this is just not your day. It is the day the trains are a bit off schedule. You fume and rage: "These —— trains are never on time," and you are late for work. Is this your excuse: "The trains were late this morning"?

If you cannot see that you were late because you did not start earlier and that you unrealistically expected everything would click, you lack overall perspective—a most necessary bit of executive know-how.

It takes more executive know-how to lead in some situations than others, but basically the distinction between "executive" (leader) and "follower" (subordinate) type of thinking is most evident in these two areas:

Perspective
Objectives

For study purpose we are assuming here an "average" or "typical" group of subordinates (not trying to look like executives!).

Now let us examine "executive" and "subordinate" thinking in terms of objectives and perspective within the framework of any company which produces a product to sell, hopefully, at a profit. Stop right there! Already all parties involved are split on goals:

The owners want a profit.
The employees want to earn a living.
The customers want the most value for the least cost.

Also every phase of the manufacturing operation has differing objectives and perspectives.

Now see how the perspective from which each person views the product varies:

The *owners* see it as the nucleus of a profitable enterprise.
The *salesmen* see it as something to sell.

The *engineers* see it as a scientific and highly technical process which they have to keep running without a hitch.

The *purchasing department* sees the product in terms of raw materials to be bought for the best price.

The *bookkeepers* see a set of figures to balance accurately.

The *shop workers* see the product as a substance to be changed by them in a certain way in order to earn their daily pay.

As you can see, the "typical" subordinate does not view his company's activities as a composite picture, but as the workday's daily events affect *him*. By direct contrast, executive know-how is the successful coalition and direction of all these differing views and objectives toward the principal goal of having the company show a profit.

You are thinking like an executive when you are aware that to accomplish this aim an organizational structure is necessary. More than that, you understand exactly what your company's structure is. This is true whether the organization is large or small. Naturally, the more people involved, the more complex the management process.

It has been contended that the largest number people can see at one time is three. When you look at five similar objects, you are likely to see two plus three. Understandably then, to perceive the overall business operation you need more than a helicopter view of the plant. The executive approach is to divide the whole into comprehensible and logical segments and by inference arrive at the complete picture.

Organizational management principles do not differ significantly from one enterprise to another. They can all be broken down into three major divisions:

Overall design (organizational structure)
Administration (direction and control)
Result checking (Profit & loss statements, product control, expenses, etc.)

The successful executive never forgets that the elements of a business unit are tangible and intangible. Tangible resources are wealth, raw materials, labor, factory and equipment. The intangibles are tastes, needs, competition, ethics, hazards, rewards, and the company's role in community affairs and government.

Suppose one of your subordinates approaches you for a raise. He complains that his earnings cannot keep up with the rising cost of living. You sympathize with him. "I know how it is," you say, but you add that you are not going to put in his request for a raise at this time. You promise to take another look at his problem at a more propitious time, and your subordinate, believing that you do not understand his needs, goes away sulking and griping.

He only sees that he did not get that raise he wanted. *You* see that the company is suffering a slight slump; that customer tastes have changed in recent weeks. *You* are aware that a competitor has successfully wooed some of your company's most faithful buyers. You don't add to the subordinate's worry by "unloading" your problems to him, and are hopeful that product improvements by your people will turn the tide of customer response once more toward your company. *Then* you will submit your subordinate's request for a raise.

Apply that same know-how to your own needs. Do you merit a raise or re-evaluation of your contributions? Unlike your subordinate, your timing will be good because *you* know that:

Company Policies Are Interrelated

The success of a manufacturing operation depends heavily upon the competency and adequacy of properly trained personnel, well oriented and performing the desired functions on schedule.

Realistic planning is therefore essential if the goods produced are to correspond to the quantities needed.

Due to such intangibles as competition, changing tastes, and substitutions, the manufacturing end of the business cannot be allowed to dictate sales, quantity, salaries, etc.

The manufacturing operation can only work with the materials purchased by the firm, and with the personnel hired, etc. Finally, it is the profit earned or lost, not the efficient operation of any specific segment of the enterprise that will determine its success or failure, as well as your compensation.

Then there are the legal policies which must conform to applicable laws, and the ethics of the company, all of which are necessarily coordinated and dependent upon each other. See? Now, you are thinking like an executive; you have the *whole picture* in focus.

ACT LIKE AN EXECUTIVE

Never underestimate the power of "snob appeal" to enhance your "executive look." No matter how much or how little authority you actually exercise, your subordinates always credit you with more. They really do not want you to be "one of them." They want and need to look *up* to you. Their attitude to management in general reflects the way they see you.

No one has done more for the "good neighbor" image of Gimbels Department Store in New York than the late Bernard Gimbel whose own image grew to be bigger than life.

Allegedly, a few years ago when Bernard Gimbel was still "keeping store" at West 33rd St., Gimbels featured an October sale of boys' bikes. A woman called the store and ordered one of the bikes to be held for her at the sale price until Christmas.

December 24th arrived, and no delivery. Frantically, the customer called everybody at Gimbels who could help her until at last she was talking to Bernard himself. Her order had been lost, and there were no more bikes. Her little boy, she said, was ill and looking forward to the bike she had promised for Christmas.

The result was dynamic. Within minutes Mr. Gimbel had called the Detroit manufacturer who vowed to put a bike on the next flight out. A few hours later Mr. Gimbel's own chauffered limousine collected the bike and delivered it in time to assure a sick little boy of a very merry Christmas. Of such stuff is a leader's *status*.

Status is just about synonymous with your "executive look" to your subordinates. The loss of status is "more than a loss of prestige; it seriously affects your personality." (From Keith Davis, *Human Relations at Work*.)

Laugh if you wish about the "status" of glass ashtrays over metal ones, curtains vs. no curtains, but these symbols are dear to the hearts of the status minded. They loudly proclaim to all that you are low or high on the totem pole, but they do not, per se, make you "look like an executive."

In one organization it is a "no status" symbol for an executive to do his own typing. Whenever there is a shortage of clerical help, the executives sneak into the office during off hours and furtively type up emergency correspondence that cannot wait.

But at another smaller company there are never enough secretaries to go around, and nobody thinks a thing about it when members of the senior staff fold back their shirt cuffs and peck at a typewriter. Even the president does it sometimes.

Your functions much more than your age or length of employment determine your status in an organization, although, all else being equal, the latter qualifications add to or diminish your status.

There is an important difference between nominal status (based upon rank) and true status (based upon competency). Whatever your title, you maintain your executive status with subordinates only as long as you demonstrate superior competence.

Status Is an Attitude—Mainly Yours

I recently moved out of a high-rise, so-called "luxury" apartment where, for a while we enjoyed the services of an excellent superintendent. An extremely competent man who performed his duties cheerfully and with dignity, this superintendent had the respect of the management, the tenants, and the maintenance crew.

After a year or so, he deservedly moved up to manager of another group of apartment houses. His successor evidently rated his status as "inferior" to that of the tenants, and tried to cover it up with a self-conscious superciliousness. He never greeted a tenant, but now and then he would condescend to perform a badly needed service.

It did not take long for the service personnel to size up their new boss, and their appraisal was all too obvious in the general breakdown of the former excellent upkeep of the premises.

As for the tenants—yes, we did "look down" on the new man, not because he was the superintendent, but because he was not a good one. As soon as leases expired, many tenants moved out.

Remember, you give status to any job you perform well.

Go Where Executives Go

Like the proverbial birds of a feather, executives flock together. It is a fact that executives enjoy each other's company better than anyone else's. That competitive trait, so much a part of a leader's make-up, carries right over into his social and leisure activities. It is no coincidence that so many leading executives excel in competitive pastimes like golf, tennis, yachting and card playing.

Away from the office the executive's natural habitat is the *club*—country, political, athletic, or university. Not infrequently business leaders belong to all of them. You will "look more executive" there if you are also proficient in one or more activities.

If not, you can still join in the "executive fun" by talking their language. That language is "shop." The almost universal absorption of business leaders with industrial matters is another bond that links executives together. They may bore their wives and "outsiders" with their favorite topic, but never each other!

In addition to the status appeal of club memberships, there is also this very practical side—you always have a suitable place to take that special client or visiting VIP, when home entertaining is not feasible, or public restaurants pall.

Don't, however, rule out your home and your wife as flattering accessories to your "executive look." A pleasant home—plus a gracious and socially acceptable wife as hostess—can add up to very effective executive know-how!

Self-Control

Self-control can do more for your "executive look" than any other single attribute.

Leaders are often lonely people; you cannot be simultaneously a leader and also a member of the herd. Like it or not your followers want to see you as a "superman" who walks in hallowed places and has none of their weaknesses or foibles. Living up to this image is not easy.

During a strike by sanitation workers in New York City, a greatly harassed Mayor Lindsay spent several turbulent and sleepless nights. At the height of it all the Mayor was recording a public statement to be aired at a later time. Right in the middle of his talk he was distracted by the entrance of someone into the studio. "Somebody shut that —— door," he is reported to have commanded angrily.

The remark was struck from the tape, and the Mayor's public image was saved, although I understand that the original recording has become a collector's item among sound engineers!

Later the Mayor apologized, declaring that if he had not been so

tired he would never have let himself go like that. It could happen
to anyone, you say, under similar provocation? That is true, but the
Mayor of New York is not just "anyone"—he cannot afford the
luxury of exploding in public. Neither can *you*, if you want to "look
like an executive."

Few "big" men can get away with temperamental outbursts.
General Douglas MacArthur could. It has been reported that his
men verily quaked at the General's blistering tirades, but they
would follow him to hell and back.

Just the same, you and I are much more likely to lose every time
we allow anger or disappointment to displace cool objectivity.
Even if you are subjected to ill-tempered criticism or unfair treatment, it is never wise to respond in kind. A "good show" as the
British say is executive know-how.

Griping has a decidedly "unexecutive look" to it; what it makes
you look like is a "sore loser." So before you jump on your subordinates or on the "system" ask yourself, "Can I do it better?" If
you can, then do it, or show others how to do it. If you can't, don't
gripe—think of a better way to do it. Finding a better way to do a
task gives you an executive look.

Instability or lack of self-control shows up in more ways than
temperamental outbursts and complaints.

Kurt Lowen, a plant supervisor, was once told "in confidence"
that a major customer was not going to renew its contract with his
company. "It looks like a layoff in the spring, but you have nothing
to worry about, Kurt," had been the parting comment. Although
personally reassured, Kurt was still worried about the well-being of
his more favorite subordinates, so he impulsively tipped them off
about the expected layoffs.

Within a very short time there began to appear signs of restless-
ness and anxiety among the alerted workers who were trying to line
up new jobs before the sword fell. Their apprehension soon
affected the quantity and quality of their production.

Then, unexpectedly one day, the important customer decided to
renew his contract with the plant, but it was too late for Lowen's
"pet" workers who had already departed.

Naturally none of this made Kurt Lowen "look like an executive" to either his superiors or his followers! Telling all is like

wearing your heart on your sleeve—it leaves you vulnerable. In managing, as in wooing, you need know-how.

Social Awareness helps you to look like an executive; the lack of it has the opposite effect.

The former president of a major company lost some valuable contracts and, subsequently, his position because he acted as he felt—no matter who was present. I once saw this socially prominent, but rude individual pour out his coffee on the tablecloth to spite the waitress who had inadvertently spilled a little coffee over onto his saucer as she carried the full cup to his table.

Although infinitely preferable to none at all, beautiful table manners and highly polished social graces do not always give you the "right executive look" either. Here again, self-control in the form of moderation is your guiding principle.

For example: Pretty good table manners make a better impression on others than an obvious fetishness which at best implies that you are overly concerned with the details of etiquette, and at worst projects an "unexecutive" subservience to conformity.

The rule of *self-control* especially applies to the telling of "dirty stories."

Earl Roberts of the General Electric Company remembers, but would rather forget, a guest speaker who drank too much just before he had to address a mixed group of clients and their wives at a social business function. The speaker started his talk by telling an "off-color" story. It was definitely not a hit, but everything might still have been all right if the young man had not gone on telling one dirty story after another.

"You could hear a pin fall in the ensuing silence," Earl recalls shudderingly, "I invited the man, and I had to apologize." Later, one sweet lady bemoaned to Earl, "To think that awful young man came from my home town." She wasn't the only one ashamed of him. Evidently the offender's boss felt the same way, because he subsequently told Earl, "That fellow will never look like an executive to me again."

As Mr. R. E. Smith, Manager of Engineering of the General Electric Company says, "The opportunities for public exposure by the average executive are few and precious." Look and act like an executive; don't waste your chances.

You always look like an executive when you make good things happen in terms of your company's objectives of showing a profit, directing a satisfied, productive work force with the least labor/management friction, and projecting the company's desired image.

You cannot make these good things happen without the proper use of your "executive tools" to help you:

> Stimulate top performance
> Stabilize emotions
> Conserve time and energy
> Obtain conformance
> Teach
> Win loyalty
> Develop
> Restrain
> Understand

Your stimulating tools are:

> *Enthusiasm* for the job at hand and for the aims and goals of your company.
> *Cheerfulness* which depends on good health, proper attitudes, and disposition.
> *Fairness* in giving credit where it is due, developing the capable subordinate, and restraining the non-conformist.
> *Diligence* in leading subordinates to stick with the job through completion.

The stabilizing tools are:

> *Calmness* when everything is not going as it should.
> *Consistency* to think before you act, but not to backtrack once you have made your decision known. Treat all subordinates fairly all the time.

The conserving tools are:

> *Orderliness* in organizing a work and time schedule for yourself as well as your subordinates.
> *Receptiveness* to suggestions by superiors and subordinates on quicker, better ways to do the job.
> *Frankness* in getting to the core of the problem without hedging by facing up to each situation honestly and now.

Persuasiveness or ability to influence others to perform smoothly and quickly.

These are your conforming tools:

Firmness tempered by prudent judgment.

Tact in dealing with others. Familiarity or indiscretion with your superiors breeds the same treatment of you by your subordinates. Another word for tact is consideration of others.

Tolerance and patience with the failings of others. Keep cool.

These are your tools for teaching others:

Open-mindedness to see the other fellow's point of view.

Communication of your ideas and those of others. Use simple direct language, keep it brief. Say what you mean and mean what you say.

Promote loyalty with these tools:

Integrity or intellectual honesty that encompasses basic honesty with the material and moral elements of life, as well as a capacity for insight into the relative merits of another's position.

Kindness and compassion for others.

Fairness in evaluating others on individual capability and performance, rather than on personal appeal.

Use these tools to restrain:

Self-control to earn and keep the respect of others.

Courtesy in dealing with your subordinates without familiarity or condescension, but with understanding.

Delegation of responsibility to capable subordinates, both for the purpose of developing their abilities and for saving you time.

The following are the understanding tools of an executive:

Insight into yourself and others. Everybody has similar needs and difficulty in communicating them.

Intelligence to perceive and understand.

Knowledge of both your job and general interest topics.

Sympathy
Humor
Remember—your own performance speaks louder than any-
thing you say—no matter how well you say it.

Review

If you are tall and slender and know that white socks don't go
with a dark business suit, you are ahead of the other fellow. But
you won't last long unless you know what else it takes to "look like
an executive." You look most like an executive when you *think* and
act like one.

You are thinking like an executive when you:

1. Know that the survival of your organization and its personnel depends upon the salability of its product or service,
   and the satisfaction of its clients' wants (including the
   creation of wants) *at prices the public will pay.*
2. Thoroughly understand the organizational structure and
   policies of your company, and *never lose sight of the whole
   picture*, even when dealing with apparent "trifles."

You can acquire executive know-how by "following the leader."
Next to actual experience, the best way to become an executive is
to observe those who have become successful in your chosen field,
and *put into practice their tested techniques*, studying everything
available on the subject and seeking counsel of experienced and
wiser heads.

Consequently you are almost certain to have the "right executive
look" when you:

Communicate effectively.
Keep abreast of technological advances.
Use the best known and proven techniques.
Recognize and concentrate on those items which produce the
profits for your company.
Develop subordinates.
Expend funds wisely.
Are creative and self-starting.
Accept responsibility for your actions and those of your sub-
ordinates.
Make intelligent decisions on facts, which can be made to
stick without reflecting adversely upon your judgment.

CHAPTER THREE

Speak Up with Confidence!

"Mend your speech a little lest it may mar your fortunes," Shakespeare (*King Lear*). If you are trying to get ahead, you know how true that is.

Self-confidence and the ability to communicate enthusiastically are the two most common attributes of successful leaders. Yet, an inestimable number of would-be (and could-be) capable executives are hidden behind an "iron curtain" of timid silence, destined to forever withhold their needed talents. Miserably tongue-tied, always frustrated, these hopefuls remain out of sight, mutely alone— and they don't have to be. That's right, their isolation is by choice, because anyone who really wants to can speak up with confidence.

For the aspiring executive isolation often spells o-b-l-i-v-i-o-n, because silence "talks." It says to superiors and subordinates, "I don't know" and "I don't care" even if you know all the answers and care very much.

Talking Is Not Necessarily Communicating

You talk to people every day, but how effectively are you doing it? Are you getting the results you want?

The president of a corporation called in his seven vice-presidents one morning to outline a change in policy and commissioned them to see that it was immediately put into practice. Soon no less than eight policies were being initiated, so the president called in the distinguished Dr. Fran Funk of Syracuse University to find out what was wrong with all his vice-presidents!

Some people are gifted with a natural facility to express themselves clearly and eloquently, but for many, effective communication is the result of study and practice. If failure to obtain the desired response has intimidated you into silence, perhaps all it takes to restore your self-confidence is some homework on:

How you say it (your tone of voice to superiors, associates, subordinates, etc.)
Your listening tolerance
Speech (enunciation, vocabulary, grammar, etc.)
Dictation techniques
Conference know-how
Your "public address" system, including the use of a microphone

How Did You Say It?

You don't want to be too democratic in the way you address one and all. It is good politics to vary your tone of voice with the recipient. For example, a subtle note of deference implying due respect generally pleases superiors and clients, but a touch of firmness and authority will win you better cooperation from your subordinates.

The Way You Give an Order Is Important. The spoken word is less tangible than the written one—you have to be more careful not to appear offensively superior or too abrupt. Face to face, your subordinate's ego and self-respect are much more on the line than in written instructions. Yet, there are times when you must say, "Do it!"

You may have heard about the worker who adamantly refused to follow directions until his boss called him and said, "Do it or you're fired." Later when someone asked him why he had not complied in the first place, the worker answered, "It was never explained like that to me before."

There is also the employee who not only has to be told what to do but must also be shown how to do it.

Mr. Dave McGonagle, Vice-President of the West Virginia Armature Company likes to tell how one of his customers complained that the bearings were falling out of rollers when they were supposed to be inserted under resistance with 60 ton presses.

Upon investigation Dave learned that a new employee was given a supply of rollers and bearings and told by the foreman how to install them with the admonition, "Let me know if you have any trouble fitting the bearings in." The bearings were undersized, and the worker discovered that he could tap them in place with his hands, eliminating the need for using the 60 ton press. After the complaints came in, his defense to the foreman was, "You said to let you know if I had any trouble, and I *didn't* have any trouble putting them in."

Give instructions in such a way that subordinates know that you mean them. In an important baseball game, the coach signaled his runner on first base to steal second base and was ignored, as were his signals to steal the next base as the player moved up to second and third base. When asked later why he didn't follow instructions, the player said, "I didn't think you meant it."

Your self-confidence can drop a notch or two when what you say is too literally interpreted. I once told a temporary assistant to do a certain task "as soon as convenient," really meaning "right away, if possible," but she did it at "her convenience" two days later.

Attitudes are hard to disguise, so if you are biased toward, or scornful of your assistant, be sure it will have a bearing on how your directions are carried out.

Try saying "we" instead of "you," when enlisting the cooperation of others. Including yourself as a member of the work team helps promote enthusiasm for the task. Your helpers will feel that they, too, share in the achievement, and the successful accomplishment of your objective becomes also their goal.

You can be more confident that your orders will be carried out as intended when you:

Are sure of your objective.
State it clearly in terms understandable to the recipient.
Show how if necessary.
Permit subordinates to ask questions.
Allow sufficient time for effective accomplishment.

Do You Listen?

Don't envy the Big Mouth—he usually fares no better than his silent opposite. In your eagerness to finally speak out, don't overlook the interdependence of listening with effective speaking. The best talkers are often the best listeners. Why? It is because you have to listen to the other person before you can establish rapport with him, and *rapport* is the key to all effective communications.

Maybe you think that listening is a natural habit that nobody has to learn, like eating or sleeping, but the fact is that most of us hear without listening. Regardless of degree of intelligence you will forget most of what you hear unless you train yourself to listen. There are many listening training programs available—some in conjunction with speech education, but basically they boil down to this: *Slow down your thinking while you listen.*

You can't "tune in" on the speaker's wave length, if you are overly preoccupied with what *you* are going to say when it is your turn to speak. Listening will help give you the insight to say the right thing. Students who fall asleep in the back of the classroom are not the only ones who give "dumb" answers.

The Reaction of Your Hearers Is Very Important

Can you predict how others will respond to what you say? This is a problem area, because it is not easy to readily discern another's attitude. You have to look for clues in their behavior as well as their speech.

Heed the old maxim: "Actions speak louder than words." Your audience may pay lip service to your suggestions, but if they are inattentive, evasive or surly, you can be sure that you are not "selling" them—they are not with you.

Take the case of the young manager who stressed "quality," "quality," day in and day out, but just as consistently let sloppy performance get by unrebuked. As soon as the workers caught on to the manager's discrepancy, his meaningless admonitions went "in one ear and out the other."

NOTE: A definite correlation exists between opinion (expressed judgment) and attitude (true feeling), but clues notwithstanding, you can never be sure of another's attitude, until you observe what he does.

It is important to know when you have lost your listener's interest, and not go on talking to no purpose. If you know how to listen and observe, you can often "feel" another's response before it is voiced.

Establish Rapport

Likeable people seldom have difficulty in putting across their ideas, but popularity is not a prerequisite for effective communication. Mutual respect is the indispensable facet for establishing rapport.

Here is how Mrs. Lillian Hermel confidently competes in the "man's world" of textile manufacturers. In trying to win over new clients Lillian frequently hears, "Why should I give you my business? I am satisfied with the service I now receive." "True," she replies, "You have a valid point there. However, I operate on a small commission and can make you a very attractive offer. Isn't it a good precaution to have a number of reliable sources of supply? Manufacturers have been known to go out of business, as my former employer did upon his retirement. Just give me a small order to show what we can do for you. I think you will be glad you did."

Lillian seldom gets "no" for an answer. Her unfailing courtesy and friendly persuasiveness are substantially supported by a thorough knowledge of her product and confidence in its quality, but her real secret of success lies in her keen knowledge of human nature.

Watch out for these meaningless gestures and irritating mannerisms which betray a lack of self-confidence and hinder rapport:

> Toying with your necktie.
> Running your fingers inside your collar.
> Tapping with a pencil or finger.
> Cracking knuckles or biting fingernails.
> Feverishly touching everything reachable.

Nobody likes a know-it-all. Take care not to goad your audience into acting counter to your expressed wishes by appearing opinionated or dogmatic. Do you state as facts your personal feelings or private impressions of the facts?

Expect to be challenged on very positive statements. Have substantiating proof to bear you out. Don't be like the lawyer who addressed the jury with the statement, "These are the conclusions on which I base my facts."

You can confidently expect to promote your ideas when you:

Are yourself (sincere, unaffected, modest).
Show unfailing courtesy.
Let others do some of the talking. (Yours is not the only point
   of view.)
Are honest.
Do not force your ideas on others.
Stick to the facts.

When Words Fail

I knew an engineer who worked for a major oil company in
Indonesia, but never learned the language. It was his responsibility
to hire a group of local workers for a certain wage per mile of area
cleared through the jungle. The natives were to remove the fallen
trees that fell into the roadway at an additional charge. Every time
such a removal was necessary, my friend and the local contractor
would engage in a frustrating harangue about summoning the
workers who always seemed to be hours away from the site.

Finally the perspiring Indonesian ran over to the oil company
bulldozer, and with much gesticulating and hand waving he went
through the motions of moving the fallen trees. After he did this a
few times, the young engineer "got the message"—it was more
practical (hence more economical) to use the company equipment
to move the heavy trees which fell into the roadway.

Language is only one communicating agent. Strategically timed,
silence is a most forceful message transmitter. Use it economically
to convey more fittingly than words: sympathy, dismay, respect,
admiration.

In reviewing the previous day's work, an English professor asked
one of his students, "What would be your reaction if you saw a
man masticating resin on the bus?" "I'd look for a policeman,"
came the unhesitating reply. The class laughed, but the teacher
said never a word—he just handed the boy a dictionary.

The right amount of silence at the right time can dramatize the
effectiveness of what you say when you do speak up.

You Can Be Articulate

"We have nothing to fear but fear itself," said President Franklin Delano Roosevelt one memorable day when this nation was
undergoing a bitter crisis. Emerson has said, "Fear defeats more

people than any other one thing in the world." A man who never knows fear is a fool, but the fear of speaking up is worse than foolish; it is fatal—to self-confidence and to progress.

A job, any job, was precious in the terrible days of the depression in the 1930's, and Fred Hoffman, salesman, was about to lose his coveted assignment.

Time after time he had been turned away by customers who never heard him out, because Fred's fear of rejection would paralyze his thinking and tie his tongue. Instinctively Fred knew that if he could only show his wares, they would "sell themselves," as they did for his fellow salesmen. It had become a contest of fears for Fred—the fear of defeat pitted against his fear of unemployment. On the morning that Fred decided to conquer his fear, he arrived early and set up his display at the receptionist's desk of a tough customer. When that surprised individual came out there were Fred's wares neatly laid out. His merchandise thus reassuringly displayed, Fred had no trouble with his "spiel." He made that sale. With this first triumph came a new surge of self-confidence that not only saved Fred's job, but also his self-respect.

Perhaps it is a harsh, shrill or monotonous tone of voice, a limited vocabulary or education, insufficient or wrong information that is shaking your confidence to speak up. You are right to be concerned about (but not afraid of) undesirable traits that can and often do adversely affect your hearers, but do you care enough to do something about correcting them?

The deft combination of *vocabulary, enunciation* and *coherence* can woo your listeners into doing your bidding without resistance. You will, therefore, need a dictionary, tape recorder and full length mirror to get the most out of your speech improvement efforts.

Read Your Way to Vocabulary Development

There is only one way to build your vocabulary—*Learn new words*—the more the better. *Reading* and more reading is the key to vocabulary development.

Lou Salinari is a successful car dealer, entrepreneur and community leader who talks interestingly and competently on almost any subject. You always know what he means because his vocabulary, while extensive, is never "over your head." He is one of the best educated and well informed men I know, and he never finished the eighth grade! How does he do it? "I read all the time, anything from Shakespeare to cereal boxes," says Lou.

"The difference between the right word and the almost right is as different as lightning and a lightning bug," said Mark Twain.

Keep a good dictionary handy—authoritative, up to date and of sufficient volume to furnish adequate information. Examine its presentation and refer frequently to its table of contents for knowledge of abbreviations, common usages, pronunciation and the origin and development of words. A good dictionary will tell you which meanings are obsolete or colloquial, and give information of the derivative nouns, verbs and adjectives.

Discover the many ways there are to say the same thing without resorting to unfamiliar usages and foreign expressions. For example, a common and very much overworked word is *skill* which is often incorrectly used to mean: aptitude, cleverness, dexterity, ingenuity, deftness, to mention some. Each of the synonyms has a slight difference of meaning which will more distinctly describe your intent.

As you master and use new words and phrases, keep alert to their context. I find the following mental teasers helpful in that evaluation:

Did Noah stand before the ark?

(Do I mean before it was constructed or in front of it?)

Would you rather a cat bite you or a dog?

(I would rather have the cat bite the dog!)

What Did You Say?

In the center of a conference room one of the group is addressing his colleagues, two of whom can be seen whispering to each other and exchanging what looks like a magazine clipping. A few seats away one member is absorbedly buffing his fingernails to a fine glow while his immediate neighbor idly doodles on his pad. Throughout the whole gathering there is much shifting of positions and crossing of knees. Yawns are barely stifled as now and then a comprehensible phrase or two is garnered from the speaker's mumbled, scarcely heard delivery. The poor man is in effect talking to himself.

And so will you, too, be talking to yourself unless you speak up *correctly, distinctly* and *audibly*. You owe your listeners—all of them—this courtesy. Deny them this tribute and they will reciprocate in kind by denying you their attention. Good diction helps you to establish rapport and is a strong confidence booster.

A pleasing enunciation is achieved by rounding out the words. Each word has its own, definite outline. Sloppy speech, such as careless slurring of words is nothing more nor less than the failure to open your mouth fully when you speak. Look in your mirror as you make a statement. Do your lips scarcely move? Many people talk between clenched teeth, hence the monotone delivery which is so common.

Now look in your mirror again, this time pronouncing the five vowels, a, e, i, o, u, as distinctly and carefully as you can.

You had to stretch your mouth and employ lips, tongue and teeth. That is the secret of good enunciation—all parts of your mouth must work.

The next step is to select a passage from a book or newspaper and record your reading of it. Play it back and listen carefully. Perhaps you are not pleased, but this is a tested method of accurately evaluating your performance. Now you know where to begin.

Don't look for instant transformation. Your efforts will bring improvement in stages. Often the change will be obvious to others before you detect it yourself.

Write down the following five ways to better speech and keep them on your mirror as reminders:

1. Breathe deeply.
2. Open your mouth wide, using tongue, teeth and lips.
3. Articulate each sound, e.g., a-lu-mi-num.
4. Keep each word separate.
5. Keep all vowel sounds pure.

Walk a Chalk Line

A farmer was once asked, "How are your crops?" "Not as good as I expected, but then I didn't expect they would," he replied.

In speech and writing coherence is a logical consistency that makes it easy for others to understand you.

I knew a man who was afraid to go fishing, because it was a "dangerous" sport. "What do you mean dangerous?" I asked. "I read where a fellow drowns once a month," was the answer. Dangerous indeed to drown once a month.

A unified communication may be obtained by following a definite plan of arrangement and excluding all irrelevant matter. In other words, coherence is the result of:

Clear thinking.
Methodical arrangement—the most important things first.
Exclusion of irrelevant matter.
Simple, direct language.

Someone once said, "First I tell them what I'm going to tell them. Then I tell them, and then I tell them what I told them." It is an excellent technique.

How Do You Rate on Dictation?

There was once an executive named Jones, who overheard a client confiding to an associate, "The next letter I get from Jones goes into the wastepaper basket. Of all the boring, trite, etc., etc., and then he seldom makes his point." Outraged, Jones immediately rushed to berate his secretary for sending out "such stupid letters." Are *you* Jones?

A surprising number of executives are Jones, overly dependent upon the skills of their secretaries to make them "look good" on paper. How much editing is your secretary doing on your communications? It is not unreasonable to expect your assistant to catch forgotten commas, omitted words, or an occasional unfinished statement, but no secretary, however competent, should be held responsible for the composition and style of your correspondence, or your spelling.

Don't blame your secretary for errors resulting from your poor dictation, insufficient knowledge of the subject or inability to make your point.

Listen to Yourself

It is time to pull out the tape recorder again. Suppose you had to take down what you are saying? Do you:

1. Pronounce the words distinctly?
2. Emphasize names, addresses, specific times and locations?
3. State your message clearly and well?

Could you write an effective letter or memo from that dictation?

With a paper explosion upon us, the private secretary is on the wane, because the more progressive firms are turning to stenographic pools equipped with high speed equipment. As the alibi of "secretary inefficiency" disappears, the executive will be evaluated by a new measure—in terms of how someone unfamiliar with his work translates what he says into a dictating machine. To meet this challenge, cultivate methodical habits of dictation.

When using a dictating machine, be sure to alert the translator to distinguish between the material to be typed and your instructions. Take a little time to plan ahead before you say, "This will be a letter, etc."

How to Make Your Secretary Love Dictation

Try these five steps to more successful dictating:

1. Visualize the entire message before you dictate the first paragraph.
2. Make notes in the margins of your letters when you read your mail. (This will save time in composing your response as you dictate, and reduces the likelihood of overlooking a salient point.)
3. Concentrate on simplicity and clarity. The shorter the better is a good rule for most business communications.
4. Stay put. Your voice "follows" you as you pace about. (Looking out the window, down into the files, etc., makes it harder for your secretary to take down your message.)
5. Give your girl a break. Unless it is really urgent (be honest, now) don't call her in for dictation five minutes before closing time, in the middle of her coffee break, or as soon as she hangs up her coat in the morning.

During unavoidable long sessions do provide an occasional pause —a smile, light comment, cold drink. Brief stops help you both to do better work. Her willingness to cooperate cheerfully with you will give you confidence in your ability to dictate effectively.

SHINE AT CONFERENCES

Business conferences are important management tools—they are also unavoidable. On the bright side, they are a wholesome change from the everyday routine.

A conference is for the purpose of exchanging ideas. That is why it is so important that you participate in the proceedings. These occasions are among your best opportunities for displaying (or hiding) your executive know-how. Do not pass them up because you are too timid to speak up. You are invited to the conference because management wants to hear your views.

Be Prepared

"Blessed is the man who, having nothing to say, abstains from giving us wordy evidence of fact." Would that this quote of George Eliot were prominently posted in every conference room and convention hall! Far better it is to keep quiet than to "shoot off your mouth" when you have nothing substantive to offer. Display enviable executive know-how by making a worthwhile contribution every time you speak up.

Seven-eighths of your self-confidence to speak up will derive from being well prepared. You know what you are talking about and this immediately conditions your hearers to respond "yes."

At a monthly conference of the Wilson Oil Products Budget Committee it was proposed that the annual budget be broken down into four three-month budgets to be reviewed and revised every three months. The whole idea was resisted by the sales department whose executives saw in this new plan a threat to their present independence, and their representative was most out-spoken in his objections. Instead of arguing with him, Mr. Worten whose "brainchild" was the proposed budget, produced charts and figures that, together with his own persuasion, convinced the dissenters that it was to their advantage to adopt the new plan.

Persuasion alone would not have done the trick here without the corroborating evidence of reports and figures, and those took homework. Try these four home rules for sprouting conference courage:

1. Study the agenda in advance. (What can you contribute?)
2. Collect more data (including exhibits or other visual aids) than you need to back up your suggestions, then trim it to fit your allotted time.
3. Arrange your ideas in orderly sequence (enumerate them as you need them).
4. Make comparisons.

What about all those good ideas you get at the oddest times? Jot them down as they occur, and on the eve of the next conference review them. If any are applicable to the matter under discussion, come out with them. Maybe they won't make an instant "hit," but if you know what you are talking about, you will at least earn the respectful attention of the others. You don't agree with everything others say either, so don't let the fear of appearing controversial force you to "clam up."

The faint-hearted and the inarticulate will find themselves mercilessly trampled underfoot by the "lions" at a conference. Don't let excessive shyness keep *you* from making a good showing.

Stand up for what you think is right, but if a counter decision becomes company policy, don't fight it—support it to the best of your ability. This is the time that being a "good loser" can make you a winner.

Remember these ten cures for conference blues:

1. Be prepared.
2. Pay close attention to the discussion.
3. Avoid side conversations.
4. Offer only relevant suggestions.
5. Bypass arguments with members or the leader.
6. Ask only questions that can be answered.
7. Yield the floor graciously.
8. Suggest solutions that can be supported with evidence.
9. Confine your remarks to the time limit. (If you only have two minutes, don't start out with historical backgrounds—get right to the point.)
10. Be sincerely enthusiastic. If you are not really sold on your own idea, be sure that your hearers will know it and irresistibly think "no" to your proposal.

Conferences are not all grim. An occasional laugh has relieved many otherwise tense gatherings. Your sense of humor can be your best ally when everything is not going your way.

When It Is Your Turn to Lead

It is not as easy as it looks to conduct a smooth running, result-getting conference. Organizational ability and a sound knowledge of human relations are the necessary assets of a successful chairman. The leader is the most important member of the conference.

The first time Leslie (now head of a large company) was asked to preside at an association meeting, he was appalled, because Wiley and Dunkin, vice-presidents of competitive firms, would be present. With good reason did Leslie quail at the prospect—both gentlemen had earned a reputation for turning meetings into mighty battles of wits. Too often the business of the day took a back seat to the lively goings-on, delighting some of the group, but exasperating the more serious-minded members. More than one experienced leader had faltered before the awesome two, and it was a critical challenge for Leslie whose only conference experience had been as a participant.

Lacking the confidence to take on Messrs. Wiley and Dunkin, Leslie talked to other leaders. He researched his topics, prepared and reprepared the agenda, and lost a lot of sleep. As a result, this is how he handled the conference:

On the big day, true to form, Messrs. Wiley and Dunkin locked horns once more, but before they had a chance to "warm up," Leslie politely intervened to state the objective of the meeting, and called upon a member of the group for pertinent information. Then every time the pair showed signs of renewing combat, Leslie, successfully hiding his nervousness, was right there between them, offering comments, and always keeping the meeting goals before the members.

There was no "show" that day. Leslie's homework had paid off, and he was on his way to the top.

Help is always available if you are interested enough to seek it. Successful experiences are the most effective of all confidence boosters.

How to Conduct a Conference with Confidence

Start small with a minimum of four to six and no more than fourteen people, because either a very small or a very large group requires the maximum leadership skill. In any size conference you have to consider the rank, competence and differences of opinion among the individuals—strive for the most compatible group possible.

Plan Ahead. What is the purpose of the meeting? Is it to be a "get it off your chest" session, the giving and receiving of information, or a developmental meeting to inaugurate policy changes? The type of conference will dictate its procedure, and it is up to you, the leader, to see that all discussions stay within the stipulated confines.

Don't ask for comments or suggestions unless you know they are desired by management, and that they will be acted upon.

At best, conferences pinpoint problems and provide workable solutions. At worst they deteriorate into aimless "bull sessions."

Mr. F. E. Brown was in great demand as a conference leader of an appliance company and often presided at the monthly supervisors' meetings at which he blocked all attempts to air trivial departmental complaints. He attributed the notably productive nature of his conferences to his technique of requiring each member to submit with his report specific, constructive recommendations.

By this ruse Mr. Brown held the meetings to a strong line of action with resultant improvements. There was simply no time for idle griping or pointless discussions.

The late William J. Donald, managing director of the National Electrical Manufacturers Association, has said that the success of a conference frequently hangs on the adroit handling of:

1. *The Person Who Talks Too Much.*
   He must be interrupted tactfully and the group invited to make remarks.

2. *The Know-It-All.*
   Convey to him that the group appreciates his broad experience, but suggest an exchange of related knowledge and experience of all members of the group.

3. *The "Heckler."*
   Keep calm and do not allow the others to become flustered. Give the heckler enough rope to hang himself. Such a person usually makes some unsound statement that will render him ineffectual for the rest of the meeting.

4. *The Grudge Bearer.*
   Steer comments away from whatever irritates this individual. (Know your group.)

5. *The Shy Member.*
   Draw him into the discussion by asking him questions that are easily answered. Express appreciation for his remarks. Let him assist with the exhibits so that he will be distracted from his self-preoccupation.

6. *The Domineering or Aggressive Individual.*
   Curb his tendency to take over the meeting by inviting opinions from the others and trying pleasantly to make him agree with you.

7. *Touchy Subjects.*
   When topics of a tender nature must be discussed, the conference leader should be neutral. As soon as possible, try to direct the group to the next subject of interest without seeming too hasty or abrupt.
8. *Holding the Group's Interest.*
   Ask questions, use exhibits and suggest new approaches when talk appears to die down. If necessary, provoke discussion by making a controversial statement.

Keep your group's attention focused on the main purpose of the gathering. Refer frequently to your agenda and be alert to small private discussions that may interfere with the orderly progress of the conference.

NOTE: The principal obligation of a conference leader is to guide, not push.

Follow Up. Use newsletters, memos and other suitable writings to prolong the otherwise short lives of spoken words. Keep fresh in the minds of the participants the results of their conference work. Follow up all decisions with the necessary written reports or announcements.

GIVE A SUCCESSFUL TALK

"There is no such animal in or out of captivity as a born public speaker." Who should know this better than Dale Carnegie whose phenomenal success was built upon this truism? Among other famous speakers, both Winston Churchill and George Bernard Shaw have confessed to experiencing paralyzing stage fright at some time in their careers.

I believe that the word "speech" is what throws most of us into a panic. There is something about that word that conjures up the formal rhetoric and studied gestures of "staged" oratory. Much of your apprehension dissolves when you start thinking in terms of talking to instead of reciting at your audience.

Audiences Are Kinder Than You Think

When my son was in the sixth grade, his class did Dickens' *A Christmas Carol* for their holiday play. The narrator was a pretty little girl whose function it was to come out before each scene and cue the audience in on the happenings. She read from a sheet, but at one time she faltered, obviously having trouble in making the words out in the poor light, said, "Excuse me," charmingly—not a bit flustered—and went over to the side of the stage where the light was better. In a matter of seconds she returned to her place and with enviable poise went on as if nothing had happened.

Children have notable stage presence and you can learn this from them: *It is not the end of the world if you make a mistake. If you don't make a big thing out of it, nobody else will, either.*

A famous orator has said that the difference between experienced and inexperienced orators is that the first have learned to make stage fright work for them. Properly controlled, apprehension can make you appear more earnest and consequently more effective. It takes plenty of practice to turn fear into an asset, and each successful talk you give will build your self-confidence and increase your platform ability. At the peak of his career, Churchill said that while he couldn't get rid of the butterflies in his stomach, he could "make them fly in formation."

You don't have to be a "great speaker" to give a successful talk.

At the annual meeting of a national trade association Mr. Y and Mr. Z, two heads of major corporations, were the featured speakers. Mr. Y's message was delivered in an audible, though matter of fact, no-nonsense voice. He raised some interesting questions, suggested possible ways and means of accomplishing the industry goals, and summed it all up neatly.

Immediately following Mr. Y was Mr. Z whose commanding stage presence was a natural accessory to his eloquence and oratory. Throughout, the audience responded to Mr. Z's wit and style with appropriate laughter or rapt attention. His theories were nebulous, the recommendations uncertain, but he finished on a high note of good humor to enthusiastic applause.

During the inevitable comments that followed, one member was heard remarking to another, "Wasn't Z's speech great? I never laughed so much."

"Well," replied his companion, "that depends upon whether you came here to be entertained or informed."

So it came to pass that long after Mr. Z's humorous talk was forgotten by the group, they were still translating Mr. Y's words into profits.

There is a big difference between talking around a conference table where you can avoid looking people directly in the eye as you collect your thoughts, and standing up to face an audience. Preparation is the secret of your self-confidence here.

Eight Hints for Preparing a Successful Talk

1. Know and research your subject.
2. Organize your presentation.
3. Look right.
4. Dress up your talk.
5. Look at your audience.
6. Practice.
7. Know when to stop.
8. Learn how to use a microphone.

Know and Research Your Subject. You must be well informed on whatever topic you speak. If you do not have a related personal experience upon which to draw, research your subject thoroughly, striving for authenticity, timeliness, and interest to the audience. On controversial matter be well versed on both sides.

Do you have the right to talk on the subject? To be convincing you should have earned the right to speak on the topic, by training, background, etc. Don't give medical advice—unless you are an M.D.

Organize Your Presentation. A speech, like a letter or report, must contain an introduction, a body, and a closing. Keep introductions simple and brief. Remember the body of your speech is the "meat" of it, or the message you wish to convey. Oratory will not compensate for insufficient coverage of your subject, so back up your point with relevant facts and convincing illustrations.

Persuade your audience to *want* to take the action you desire.

Personalize the situations whenever possible from real life experiences. Draw upon your personal repertory of friends, acquaintances and events to dramatize your message.

Only include jokes or humorous anecdotes when they fit right into your speech—this isn't very often. Dangling stories "give away" the inexperienced speaker.

Look Right. Exude confidence without cockiness. Your appearance, mannerisms, voice (range and pitch), enunciation, choice of topic—even attitudes—all add to or distract from the effectiveness of your speech. See yourself as your audience does with the help of a tape recorder and full length mirror. There are now video recorders that allow you to see and hear yourself on television.

Unusual dress, annoying habits, and strident tones all work to capture the audience's interest when they should be listening to your message.

Dress Up Your Talk. Properly used exhibits can make your speech more dramatic and at the same time give you something to do with your hands. The act of illustrating will help you keep your mind off yourself. You will be more natural.

Be careful not to block or impede the viewer's sight of the exhibits, and look at your audience all the time.

Arrange beforehand the order of presentation so that you may move smoothly from one exhibit to the next.

Put aside any props as soon as you have finished with them. Don't you hate to see a speaker fumbling with his exhibits, notes, etc.?

Look at Your Audience. Reading exclusively from your notes is about as bad as delivering a memorized speech. Both methods are likely to result in a stilted, uninteresting delivery.

Don't apologize when you must read a manuscript (on lengthy or highly technical subjects). Do so confidently. Just remember to look up at your audience frequently.

Practice. Whether or not you read your speech, practice in front of a mirror. Do you:

> Frequently look up from your script?
> Notice when your delivery is becoming monotonous?
> Mark your manuscript at appropriate spots with reminders to look up or change your inflection?
> Pause slightly after making a noteworthy comment to give your audience a chance to absorb it?
> Stand erect, but not stiffly?

Now present your talk to the mirror again, and again—until you are confident, but stop practicing before your delivery becomes wooden.

I know an executive who has become a very competent speaker, much in demand for fund raising and other campaigns, who once gave us a harrowing ordeal. Because of his considerable knowledge he had been asked to give us a talk on industry problems.

Carried away by his desire to make a good showing, he carefully rehearsed his speech, memorizing it word for word. Came the fateful moment and the poor man drew a blank. Completely forgetting the opening lines of his talk, his mind could not bridge that awful gap to the rest of his material. Humiliated, he had to withdraw to be hurriedly and ignominiously replaced by an impromtu speaker.

Several practice sessions are preferable to one very long one. Rehearse just enough to build self-confidence. You want your talk to appear "easy" and natural.

Know When to Stop. Many otherwise effective talks flounder at this point. It is preferable to simply stop when you have completed your message than to grope visibly for an ending. Now is the time to make your final pitch. Ask your audience for whatever response you seek—organize, contribute, buy, build, work, etc. A brief summary of the main content of your talk is an effective close to the long speech. A thought-provoking commentary or suitable quotation can also be effective, but don't overdo it.

Learn How to Use a Microphone. The microphone can be your friend or foe. At a meeting of the International Association of Electrical Inspectors in Atlantic City, New Jersey, the microphone in the convention hall suddenly went on the fritz, and had to be disconnected to avoid the "screeching howls." But the principal speaker kept talking into the "dead" mike, hoping that it would come back on—few heard what he said. The next speaker pushed the mike aside and talked up so that more than 1,000 heard every word, thereby "upstaging" the main speaker.

The first time you use a microphone you may be startled to hear your voice coming back at you, and when you become used to the echo, you will have a tendency to shout into the instrument. Blasting your audience out of its lethargy is not the best way to set them up for a favorable response to your message.

It takes practice to master the microphone, but if you learn to treat it respectfully, you will find it a valuable confidence promoter. Remember these microphone *do's:*

Do test the microphone before the big event.
Do use your (turn down to low) normal tone of voice—your friend, the microphone will amplify the sound.

Do direct your voice slightly off-center and move back when
you are going to raise your voice.

Do stand on your own good feet without hugging (that's *too*
friendly) or leaning on the instrument.

Do be prepared for everything to go wrong, and if you have to
do without the mike, look at it this way—you might have
used it for a crutch instead of speaking up.

NOTE: An audience always loves to see a speaker overcome platform difficulties.

It's Not Hard to Speak "Off the Cuff"

The occasions for talking extemporaneously normally will far
outnumber the times you have to deliver prepared formal speeches.
Every day you are asked to express your views on one subject or
another to one or more people at a time; how well you respond
depends on your ability to think on your feet.

Involve Your Audience. I remember when Pete Healey was
asked to "Give us a few words" at a dinner party of about 20
people. Taken by surprise (nobody had asked him to prepare a
talk) the young executive arose, slightly flustered. Almost immediately a smile crossed Pete's face as he referred to his predecessor's
remarks on statistics and their role in modern business, especially,
he added, in aptitude and personality testing.

"Let me give you nice people here a little test," Pete said.
Whereupon he tore some sheets out of a small memo pad and
passed them around. "Draw four figures: a circle, a square, a
triangle, and a reverse Z. When you have finished check the one
you like best. No fair looking at your wife's entry. Now, fold them
up and give them back here for a true character analysis. You, Bill,
help me open them up."

Seconds later Pete announced, "You'll all be happy to know that
you are a very sexy, learned bunch indeed. Eight of you checked the
circle for sex orientation, seven the triangle for braininess, three
preferred the reversed Z for imagination and two of you checked
the square, indicating common sense and stability. So overall this
would be an ideal group with whom to be marooned on a desert
island. For that matter, it's a good group anywhere."

Everyone enjoyed the short interlude or filler, including the
speaker who had started out with some misgiving.

When speaking "off the cuff," it is very important to capture your hearers' attention immediately, and if possible get them to participate. Personalize, including when, where, why, how, and the result. If feasible ask questions of the audience.

What do you talk about when no specific topic is suggested? Talk about your audience and the occasion that has brought all together. If you were listening to those who stood up before you, you can readily seize upon something they said and add your own personal touch. Compliment a previous speaker if you can.

Your hearers expect you to speak with authority. This means you must know about many subjects. You store up your knowledge by continually reading, observing and listening. No matter how old you are, your education is never finished. A friend of mine who is never at a loss for the right thing to say once told me: "The 'impromptu' talk is not impromptu at all. Years of preparation have preceded every effective 'off the cuff' speech I have ever made."

The knowledge and experience to speak convincingly on many topics no one can give you, but the following pointers can make you more confident to speak up on demand:

1. Start by relating a personal experience relevant to the question, mentioning time and place.
2. Make your point briefly and enthusiastically.
3. In small gatherings include your audience, mentioning names when possible.
4. Be sincere in expressing appreciation, condolences, congratulations, etc.

I admit that all this sounds easier than it really is, and I wish there were a magic formula for instant success in "off the cuff" speaking. The hard fact is, however, that ease and confidence in spontaneous talking come only from practice—lots of it.

Look for "No-Risk" Opportunities to Speak Up. Don't leave a PTA or other meeting without getting up to say something. If you did your homework before going, be confident that you will say the right thing. From standing up to speak out of a group, it is but one step to facing an audience from a platform.

If you don't feel confident, then act confident.

With the courage to speak in public comes an added bonus of overall self-confidence that carries over into every phase of your activities.

Lean on these twelve confidence boosters for the courage to speak up on all occasions:

1. Know what you are talking about.
2. Be yourself.
3. Speak distinctly.
4. Be considerate of your listeners. (Watch your appearance and hygiene.)
5. Look pleasant.
6. Keep calm. (Avoid arguments and heated discussions.)
7. Admit it if you are wrong.
8. Be specific—especially important in order giving.
9. Include your audience whenever possible.
10. Stick to the topic.
11. Be animated. (Use facial expressions, voice inflection, and natural gestures.)
12. Use illustrations, a pertinent experience, etc.

Review

Effective communication is the lifeline of management—employment, compensation, supervision, organization, sales, purchases, etc. Specific ideas and wishes must be transmitted to others without loss or change in meaning.

If you shy away from speaking up when necessary, you are faltering in your executive role, and leaving the field of success wide open to those who can and will competently present their views to others.

Public speaking cures timidity and builds overall self-confidence.

The shy individual who wishes to get ahead must seek out every opportunity to enjoy successful experiences at speaking up.

If you now lack this confidence, you can get it.

Study human nature to help you to establish the necessary rapport with others. You have communicated effectively when your audience understands your intent.

It's not always your subordinate's fault when your instructions are not carried out to your satisfaction. Examine your order-giving technique—a change may be in order.

Communicate all the time—with your superiors, your subordinates, associates and clients in an ever improving manner. Adapt your approach and tone of voice to your audiences and talk to or with them, but not at them.

The same words often mean different things to different people, and can be further misleading if the phrasing is not correct.

All parties to a communication are alternately senders and receivers of messages, whether of words or impressions.

Timing has much to do with the effectiveness or lack of it in a communication. Wrong time and wrong place can make anything you say the wrong thing.

Your ability to be convincing is tied to your capacity for distinguishing between facts and opinions.

Timidity, sloppy speech construction, improper diction, harshness or shrillness of tone, as well as incorrect grammar, and stage fright—all yield satisfactorily to patient treatment.

Confidence to speak up on demand comes from knowing that you are going to do and say the right thing at the right time.

CHAPTER FOUR

Give Your Writing Sales Appeal

If the written word has been your nemesis, why don't you try a new approach. Think of business writing as a sales technique. You are the salesman; your reader is the customer. You are trying to sell him something. It may be a product, often it is an idea or project, and always you are selling *yourself*.

Think that your customer (reader) is also in the market for something. Sometimes he does not even know what he wants until you have "sold" it to him. Now, there is no trick to selling your customer what he wants and needs, but it takes *sales appeal* to sell him your objective.

Selling to your public is harder when you must write your "sales pitch" because you have to compensate for lack of facial animation and vocal inflection which can mean as much, sometimes more, than what you say. Neither can you answer on-the-spot questions that may arise, thereby making advance planning of your presentation more important.

Go on the premise that readers are a self-centered lot, always thinking of themselves. They want to fulfill *their* desires, solve *their* problems, not learn about *your* troubles. Every time you overlook this essential factor, you lessen your "sales appeal" for obtaining the response you seek.

The most effective business communication is the one that is thoroughly understood, and then carried out as the author intended. In other words, the writer must sell his intent.

Put Sales Appeal into Your Writing

1. Know what you are talking about.
2. Tune in on your reader's interest.
3. Be enthusiastic about your topic.
4. Zero in on your target.
5. Develop a winning style.
6. Care about appearance.

KNOW WHAT YOU ARE TALKING ABOUT

What are the facts? Answer *who, what, when, where, how* and *why.* Distinguish between *things* (objects and events) which are perceived by the five senses, and *ideas* (concepts) about which we can only have opinions. In the first you are dealing with fact, and in the second you are conveying intentions or opinions which may or may not be logical to your reader.

Carelessly intermingling things and ideas generally creates confusion, in turn, producing undesirable results. Observe:

Dear Sir:

We find it hard to believe your assertion that our clothes dryer recently installed in your home did not live up to our advertising claims. If the problems you described were caused by faulty manufacture or design, it seems to us that we would have received other complaints. Your dryer was evidently poorly installed, or there is some other explanation why you are not receiving the desired performance.

Very truly yours,

Examine the foregoing letter for words like "if," "believe," "seems," and "evidently." All express opinions that are not supported by facts, but are expressed as facts. The inept jumbling of facts and opinions cost this appliance dealer a very good customer. There is no surer way to antagonize your reader than not knowing what you are talking about.

An orderly process of thinking through will help you straighten out your thoughts and present them in an orderly and coherent fashion. Before writing any important communication, try putting down your ideas along these lines:

1. What am I promoting (ideas, plans, products or service)?
2. What is the overall promotional objective (business promotion, improved human relations, cost reduction, quality control, value analysis, etc.)?
3. What specific promotion is under consideration (brochure, lecture, meeting, product)?
4. What is the objective of the promotion (education, explanation, mind preparation, etc.)?
5. Who is my reader (type, background, viewpoint, attitude, location, etc.)?
6. What response do I desire (buy, understand, cooperate, entertain, stimulate, etc.)?
7. When and how will it be accomplished (by whom and under what circumstances)?

Now separate those elements relating to facts from intentions (wishes, desires, opinions, beliefs, etc.). Whenever possible, avoid including facts and intentions in the same communication, and never mix them up.

See how this technique helped to draw a committee's attention to the salient considerations for a proposed industry motion picture with the following questions:

> Why is there a need for an industry-sponsored film on fire alarm systems?
> Who will be the audience?
> What is the message to be conveyed?
> Who will produce the film and at what cost?
> When can the film be ready?
> How should the project be financed?

The results were immediate and positive.

TUNE IN ON YOUR READER'S INTEREST

Who is your reader? What do you know about his needs, temperament, status, prejudices, etc.? Your relationship with your reader is very important. Upon this depends the amount or lack of formality required—always more formal up than sideways or down. Your superiors are more likely to react unfavorably to slang, abbreviations, contractions, etc. than your peers.

Do not write the same letter to the druggist in a Western drug store that you would direct to the head of a large pharmaceutical agency in Los Angeles or Chicago. Similarly, your communication will lack sales appeal if you use the same approach with women as with men, where sex is a factor. Since most of your company's clients tend to fall into a general category, you should be able to appraise your reader in terms of:

Who he is.
How he feels about the problem.
How to establish rapport with him.
What suggestions are practical.
How to talk his language.
When you should communicate.

Watch out for the language barrier. Executives have above-average reading comprehension and very high capacity in their specialized field. The average reading norm has been figured roughly to be at the ninth or tenth grade level, so go easy on those technical terms, foreign expressions or unfamiliar words. Stoop without patronizing.

Mr. J. L. Gerber, manager of an electrical contracting company, recalls an unnerving experience of running almost head-on into a large electric motor placed in the entrance to his office. This was the way Mr. Gerber's new worker had interpreted his request to take the machine "out of service." Unfamiliar with the industry jargon, the worker did not know that Mr. Gerber only wanted him to cut off the power.

Don't kid yourself that the mere writing down of directions guarantees successful execution.

The day before the grand opening of his new donut shop, Mr. Henderson left written instructions to his baker to prepare five hundred dozen donuts of several varieties. Upon his return the next morning, he found the 6,000 fresh donuts, but all one kind. "Can't you read?" he stormed at the baker. "I no can read," came the aggrieved reply. All he had understood was the number of donuts to be made.

One incongruous or false note can ruin the effect you are trying to make. It is risky to be a "funny guy." Levity or flippancy are *always* out of place in serious communications (condolences, formal reports, regrets, etc.). Know your reader before you make jokes.

BE ENTHUSIASTIC ABOUT YOUR TOPIC

Don't expect to sell your reader on an idea or project about which you have a "take it or leave it" attitude. Show you care! The following letter evoked unprecedented mass attendance at the meeting, and was followed by dramatic action. Why?

Gentlemen:

The next meeting of your Committee, scheduled for December 7–8, 1966, at _____ provides an opportunity for you to serve your company and your industry, while benefiting personally.

The challenge for an industry solution as given to you by the _____ Group can be viewed in no other light. You are asked to display technical competency, yet demonstrate flexibility during the negotiating session. It is, therefore, important that you come to the meeting well prepared to articulate your point of view.

Seldom is more asked of anyone participating in our activities, and I personally look forward to your deliberations.

Sincerely yours,

The above communication is brief, to the point, and appealing, but the writer's own enthusiasm for his intent was its main selling feature.

Project enthusiasm by:

Using forceful, steamlined phrasing that moves steadily to a climax.

Accentuating the positive. Stress what to *do* rather than don't.

ZERO IN ON YOUR TARGET

The writer is often an intruder—you invite yourself into your reader's private domain. You have no idea what mood he is in when he reads your communication. To hold his attention, you must have something to say that matters to him, and you have to say it soon. Your message is not his only business for the day.

You can give *sales appeal* to any communication by a simple procedure of getting to the point, and sticking to the facts.

The Case for Brevity

When I started out, I was addicted to the folksy approach and would send out long newsy letters, taking many sentences to make my point and then floundering about trying to find a graceful conclusion. In streamlining my correspondence, I was a bit apprehensive at first at its seeming terseness, but the results have only been good.

Be Clear and Straightforward

Too often an executive who can talk his way straight to the point with commendable economy of words gets hopelessly bogged down when he writes. The results are often as unfortunate as this actual example: "I wish to inform you, that as a result of the tabulation of the letter ballots that I have received from all of you, the proposal that the industry provide the funds necessary to finance sending a delegate to the international meeting on ——, has been approved."

All that to say: "The proposal to send a delegate to the international meeting on —— is approved."

Keep it simple. Imagine that you are sitting across the table from your correspondent talking to him. Would you ever say, "Upon receipt of your letter I noted with interest, etc."? Then write as you would say it.

I know an executive who received complaints about his long-winded letters. It then took him three pages to explain why he had to write long letters. Are you using too many words to say what can be better expressed with one, such as:

be in a position to	for	can
due to the fact that	"	because
for the purpose	"	to
along the lines of	"	like
at the present time	"	now
in view of the fact that	"	since
for the period of 12 months	"	for a year
in the amount of	"	for
in the year (state, city, etc.)	"	in—

You can further condense your writing by combining short sentences, shortening a long sentence, reducing it to a clause, a clause to a phrase, etc.

For example:

The electrician came and inspected the wiring.
The electrician inspected the wiring.
He was a worker who took great care.
He was a careful worker.
That was an order that could be executed with ease.
That was an easily executed order.

Say What You Mean

At the Highland School in Jamaica Estates, New York, the ninth grade was asked to write a composition on the topic: "If you had all your priceless possessions taken away from you, which would you want back?" One answer was, "I would like to have my parents back, because they take care of me from infantry to adultery."

In their remarkably sophisticated little publication, "Laughing Stock," these children also point out that malapropisms are cute issuing from the mouths of children, but very unbecoming to adults who should know better.

So many English words have more than one meaning—if you are not careful, some of your statements may come out like this church announcement: "Men will be baptized at the North end of the church, and the women at the South end. Children will be baptized at both ends."

All misunderstandings are not funny. Take the prescription: "Take 1 whenever pain occurs."

Unfortunately, the druggist failed to specify not to exceed 6 in any 24-hour period.

In another instance, one of our staff was asked to clarify the intent of a certain paragraph. When he proceeded to add further details, he met vigorous objection. All they wanted was an explanation of the questionable passage, not the presentation of new material.

How to say what you mean:

1. Make each word the exact one needed. A noun should name a certain someone, not just anyone. Have each verb tell a specific action.
2. Be accurate about information, spelling, grammar and punctuation.
3. Illustrate when necessary, with charts, pictures, tables, etc.

DEVELOP A WINNING STYLE

In business writing, accuracy and persuasiveness are generally more important than "creativeness," but this does not mean that your communications must be dry and lifeless. Yes, you can be businesslike with style! Why then, are you hiding your desired image behind old-fashioned, ineffectual writing that has no sales appeal?

Review Your Past Performance

Go through your files and pull out some of those old memos, reports, and letters to see how they have stood the test of time. Are they still readable, i.e., expressive, informative and persuasive? Do they "sell" your message concisely? If your impulse now is to light a match to them, it is time to think of style in terms of *readability*.

Learn from the "Pros"

Borrow a few techniques from the professional writers' bag of tricks. Here are some "Inside Tips" to more readable writing:

To interest:

1. *Increase Your Vocabulary*
   Don't overwork the same old stock of words and phrases. Avoid such expressions as:

   > Yours of the 2nd
   > Beg to advise
   > Will send same
   > Contents duly noted

2. *Use Repetition Only for Emphasis*
3. *Occasionally Shift Subordinate Phrases or Clauses to the Beginning*
4. *Mix Up Simple and Complex Sentences.* Use an occasional short sentence among long ones.
5. *Now and Then Wake Up Your Reader with an Appropriate Question.*

To inform:

1. *Break Your Paragraphs Logically,* rather than whenever they "look better." A paragraph is finished when a thought sequence is completed.

2. *Use a Separate Paragraph for Each New Topic.*
3. *Include All Necessary Pronouns, Except for Telegrams.*
4. *Keep Sentences Short* enough for the reader to quickly grasp the point without omitting necessary details.
5. *Use Correct Grammar and Punctuation.* You can see that, "No, price too high" is not the same as, "No price too high."

To persuade:

1. *Place Modifiers Knowingly.* Descriptive words like "alone," "almost," "only," "just," "ever," and "before," when skillfully located, can add limitless shades of meaning. Play around with these and see.

   NOTE: He *took* it. He *took only* it. He *only took* it. *Only he* took it.
2. *Begin and End* paragraphs with your most important remarks. These are all some people read.
3. *Carefully Inject Humor.* Know your reader well, and watch your timing with this technique.
4. *Compare and Contrast.* Make your point and then back it up with facts (direct quotes, case histories). Give both sides of a controversy, but make *your case* more convincing!

CARE ABOUT APPEARANCE!

Eye appeal contributes enormously to the successful "sale" of any written message. A badly soiled chart was once returned to me with bitter comments from an offended client. Although the disgruntled recipient sullenly acknowledged the possibility that the chart was soiled in transit, he never could hide his apparent scorn for our "sloppy housekeeping."

Expect hastily scribbled notes on scraps of paper, unintelligible memos that have been unskillfully "streamlined," abundant erasures, etc., to receive the scant attention they merit.

It is easier to sell your objective to the reader when you care about:

1. *Neatness*
2. *Quality and Nature of Stationery*—Always appropriate to type of communication.

3. *Arrangment on Page*—Spacing, double spacing where feasible, margins, etc.
4. *Accuracy of Details*—Correct address, punctuation and spelling of names, use of proper titles, etc.
5. *Length of Paragraphs*—Try short introduction, heavier middle, brief closing unless one short paragraph will suffice.
6. *Brevity*—Many business communications can be effectively confined to one typed page.

NOTE: Elite type helps you to say more in the same space, but it can also destroy the "sales appeal" of your message when long paragraphs are unrelievedly crowded together.

Your Letters Are You

Letter writing is a personal form of communication that, more than any other, projects your personality, and is, therefore, a critical communication tool. Your letters can sell your company and project your desired image or they can do the opposite. In addition to the foregoing sales appeal techniques, here are four additional aids to effective letter writing:

1. Handle complaints with kid gloves.
2. Remember the thank you's.
3. Respect company letterhead.
4. Reply soon.

HANDLE COMPLAINTS WITH KID GLOVES

Calmness and courtesy are the two noticeable conditions that should prevail in dealing with clients' gripes. Remember that the customer is always right, so you need kid gloves, not boxing mitts, to assuage those bothersome complainants.

How to Do It

Act Promptly. "Sitting on" complaints will only add to the grievance of the offended person.
Be Affirmative. Discuss the constructive aspects of the complaint. Do not reopen the wound by quoting from his letter.
Give Assurance. Indicate the action that is to be taken.
Thank the Complainant. You are happy to have this occasion to review with him your company policies, and you appreciate having the matter brought to your attention, etc.

For example:

> Dear Mrs. Adams:
> Thank you for the prompt notification that your bedspread was torn in shipment.
> We do our best to prevent such damage, but are always glad to make appropriate adjustment when such accidents are called to our attention. Consequently, we are sending you a replacement shipment which should reach you within the week.
> We truly regret the inconvenience you have suffered, and we will take the matter up with our shipper to see what further steps can be taken to assure that our customers receive their merchandise in satisfactory condition.
>
> Very truly yours,

THANK YOU'S MAKE FRIENDS

Letters of appreciation, congratulations, seasonal greetings and the like are simple, inexpensive goodwill sellers. Be as quick to acknowledge small orders from old customers as you do the first large orders from new clients.

RESPECT COMPANY LETTERHEADS

As a member of the corporate family, you share in the status of your organization, but curb any impulse to use the weight of that status to obtain a personal objective. It is always risky to "lend" the name of your firm or to imply its support through the use of its letterhead stationery.

A young executive with a hotel chain in Chicago had a complaint about a major appliance in his home, and felt that his blast to the manufacturer would be more effective on the hotel stationery. I don't know whether or not the manufacturer honored the complaint, but he did cancel a major convention that had been scheduled at the hotel. It took much effort on the part of the hotel management to "square away" the ill will caused by the unauthorized use of the hotel letterhead.

REPLY SOON

You do not sell goodwill to readers who have been kept waiting for answers to letters or orders. Quickly reply to all letters, *immedi-*

ately follow up delays in shipments, notices of goods out of stock, changes in plans, etc.

My business often keeps me away from the office for long periods of time, necessitating delays in answering some communications. At such times, my secretary acknowledges the various correspondence, and where she is unable to answer in detail, advises that I will follow up by such and such a date.

Write Better Reports and Memos

Reporting is a necessary management device for long-term planning, performance evaluation, cost-cutting, and transmitting information of special significance. Reports also serve as permanent records of events that may influence future developments; and are written, oral or a combination of both. More specifically, reports are:

> *Factual*—Presenting the bare facts of an operation, observation, etc., with no comments.
>
> *Analytical*—Detailed explanation, including proffered suggestions and conclusions.

Factual reporting need not be tactless reporting!

Mr. Lee Knox, the secretary for a standing committee, had the unpleasant duty of recording the company demotion of one of the members of the group. Not wanting to cause discomfort to the down-graded member, Mr. Knox simply listed the names of all those present with their respective titles. In this way, the information was immediately available to all, without calling any undue attention to the person in question.

The *Analytical* report on the other hand is a challenging task, requiring a preparatory outline along these general lines:

> Title
> Foreword
> Body
> Conclusions (when appropriate)
> Exhibits
> Appendix or Table of Contents (for lengthy reports with lists of references, sources, etc.)

After you have assembled your report, check it carefully for readability. You can make a very long or complex report more "palatable" with these techniques:

Use headings and subheadings to highlight important points.

Deeply indent significant passages so that they "come up out of the page" at the reader.

Maintain a logical sequence—trip reports lend themselves nicely to a chronological order.

Memos are a convenient method of conveying interoffice communications and are usually informal. Like letters, they bear the stamp of the author's personality. Compact meaningful memos can convincingly sell your merits to a superior.

As in all communications, the main objective of your memorandum is to obtain a favorable response, so:

Be sure of your facts and be careful to include all important information.

(It is surprising how frequently secretaries for meetings forget to include themselves among those in attendance.)

Make your memos brief and to the point, with no room for misunderstanding.

Time, place and date are extremely important in memos and reports. Omission of any one can create confusion as well as ill-temper and strained relations. Once twenty members of a manufacturing group turned up in Chicago for a meeting that was being held in New York City.

The Codes and Standards Committee of a national trade association is in the habit of holding two-day meetings. On one occasion, Mr. W. F. Seubert, then of The Arrow-Hart & Hegeman Electric Company planned to attend the second session, but found himself to be the only one present. The meeting had adjourned by staying in session longer than normal on the first day, and no one had remembered to inform the "latecomer" who had advised that he would be present on the second day.

NOTE: More formal memoranda are assembled on special paper, and will frequently require you to reach conclusions and make recommendations. All will be tactful and courteous in tone.

Helpful Reminders

WHY ARE YOU WRITING THIS?

Keep in mind economy of effort and break problems down into principal parts. When you are not sure of your objective, you may find yourself submitting several follow-up reports when one good one would suffice. Think through before you start.

Where Is It Going?

Up, across or down? If up, do your superiors require lots of detail? Are tables, graphs, charts, etc., appropriate? Should you make recommendations? Until you know these answers, you should proceed with caution, measuring reactions for your future guidance.

How Long?

The subject of your report and the amount of time your reader has should determine the length of your report. Too long is the common error, yet your reports should be clear, accurate, sufficient and interesting. Neither underestimate the importance of a problem nor make mountains out of mole hills. Practice and care will help you make the correct analysis.

Take the Easy Way

You don't have to be "original" about everything you write. Save your "style" for those occasions requiring that extra touch of sales appeal. For routine communications, take these short-cuts:

Utilize all available duplicating processes like printed forms, stamped return envelopes, etc.

Save time by "selling" your intent the first time.

Be choosy about your correspondents. Don't waste your company's money and time chasing blind leads.

Don't write when an inexpensive phone call will do.

Review

The written word is only one of the many ways you use to sell your purpose and yourself, but selling is a one-way street, unless your reader "buys." Even a genius can thoroughly conceal natural abilities with poor writing and inept presentation of his ideas.

Sincerity, directness, comprehension and interest add up to *"readable"* writing. Readability contributes the most *"sales appeal"* because it nets you better results faster.

What is your "pitch"? Writing with sales appeal can help you to successfully:

Respond to needs and questions of others

Innovate desired changes

Show appreciation
Coordinate
Motivate
Discipline, direct and control
Instruct
Reward
Establish authority
Implement
Influence
Inform
Involve
Gain cooperation
Reassure and promote self-confidence
Remind
Report
Assess and evaluate

Result-getting business communications are:

Brief but cover all relevant factors
Understandable
Substantive (things and facts are separated from intentions, ideas, concepts and opinions)

CHAPTER FIVE

Take the Fear out of Decision Making

"Who is afraid to make decisions," quipped the young executive starting on his first supervisory responsibility, "I'm afraid to make mistakes!" Isn't everyone?

Yes, decision making is inherently risky. We all know that decisions have a nasty habit of sometimes ricocheting, knocking their authors right out of the executive running. So it is not only reasonable to treat decision making with a healthy respect; it is the intelligent thing to do.

The realistic executive expects trouble. If he is also capable, he "keeps his cool" and tries his best to solve his problems methodically, unlike the incompetents who plunge in recklessly or panic when compelled to make a decision.

The exceptional leader does more than that—he *thrives* on problems. To him, decision making is the elixir of his life, an exciting challenge that takes the "ho-hum" out of his working day.

What is the significant difference between all types of leaders? The difference is in their approach to decision making. Obviously, leaping without looking or worrying fruitlessly are not methods conducive to successful problem solving. Both the capable executive and the outstanding leader share in common a readiness for emergencies and a calm orderly approach to decision making; the latter just enjoys it more!

One Good Decision Does Not a Leader Make. The man who stays on top not only loves to make decisions, he has also developed the *habit of making right decisions.*

95

This know-how is not too hard to come by, because most big decisions grow out of little ones. As Mr. R. F. Waldrop, Executive Vice-President of Millbank Manufacturing Company, shrewdly observes: "There is no such thing as a single decision—every major decision is built upon subordinate decisions."

The now historical and strategic Suez Canal was seventeen years fermenting in the brain of the young French diplomat, Ferdinande de Lesseps before it became a major decision. Then it took yet another ten years and many more decisions for the Suez Canal to emerge into the engineering and controversial marvel that we know today. The whole story is not yet told.

How big a part does luck play in making the "right decision"? People and circumstances can just as unexpectedly work for you as against you. Yet, sometimes what passes for "luck" is nothing more nor less than know-how based upon shrewd judgment and careful timing. The absence of "luck" can just as easily add up to "fate."

Contrary to his modest assertion, it was surely more than luck that enabled the famous J. Paul Getty, business wizard and renowned author to make the string of right decisions that secured for him control of the Tidewater Associated Oil Company.

In one of his articles he confessed that his early wildcatting background gave him a knowledge of oil wells that was no small factor in his initial successes.

Successful leaders have a decision-making "system." And while there are no techniques, however effective, that will yield the right decision every time, there *is* a way to take the fear out of decision making. It can almost be summed up in a single word—*order*. That's the secret of the following five way plan to better decisions or how you can learn to love decision making:

1. Organize Yourself
2. Welcome Responsibility
3. Master the Techniques of Problem Solving
4. Create a "Success Climate"
5. Learn from Mistakes

Organize Yourself

Many people shy away from problem solving for one reason only: they are disorganized.

Intuitively many disorganized persons, sometimes without ever identifying their reason, sense that there is "something wrong" about their whole approach. They are right. Disorderliness contributes to chaos—it interferes with straight thinking.

Justly or unjustly, it is only reasonable (and common), therefore, to attribute to the disorganized person inability to make wise decisions.

If you have not already done so, perhaps the best decision you will ever make is the one to organize yourself.

The organized executive:

> Gets *more* done.
> Does a *better* job.
> Finishes his task *sooner.*
> *Foresees* the outcome.
> *Makes wiser decisions.*

A desk piled high with work does not prove that you are a busy executive; more likely it denotes that you are disorganized!

After 20 years, Clyde Smith is still a minor executive in his company. He works hard, often putting in long hours. Sometimes you can hardly see Clyde around or above the pyramids on his desk, which is just as well, since he usually works at an empty desk somewhere else.

Nobody is surprised that Clyde sometimes mislays necessary documents. Once he "lost" an important letter only to have it reappear weeks later—too late for the required action.

It looks like Clyde is good for another 20 years in his present post.

I was once in the same boat as Clyde. For economic reasons there was not sufficient staff to send out communications as fast as they came into the organization. I soon had an untidy stockpile of mail and other papers cluttering my work area. Necessity compelled me to come up with a system whereby I could locate the needed document "when the heat was on." I obtained a rack and set up 40 file folders on my desk. The piles of material in my area were sorted and placed into their appropriate folders.

Through this procedure, the material was screened with about ⅓ discarded immediately. As new material came in, it was sorted and filed in the order of its importance.

Don't let disorganization "foul up" your decisions! Try these five ways to greater efficiency:

1. Plan a work schedule and stick to it.
2. Do the most important or difficult things first.
3. Make small decisions promptly and positively.
4. Use all available help.
5. Learn to say "no."

SCHEDULE YOUR WORK

You've heard, "The more important a man is the less work he does." Nowadays it is correct to say, "The more important a man is the less *routine* work he does."

How much time are *you* spending on mundane details that others could do, perhaps better?

Keep track for one day of how much time you spend on:

> Executive functions (planning, organizing, delegating, attend·ing meetings, conferences, etc.).
> Routine duties (correspondence, dictating, telephone calls, etc.).
> Visiting.
> Overtime (both at home and in the office).
> Lunch, coffee breaks, etc.

If your finding is, "too much on the last four and not enough on the first," it may be because you are not giving priority to what is most important.

DO THE MOST IMPORTANT THINGS FIRST

Efficiency requires that you do this and then proceed according to degree of urgency. You may be surprised to find how often you change your mind about what is really necessary.

Priority determination can be difficult, not so much because you do not know what to do first, but because you really do not want to do it. Your ability to make the proper distinction between these two can result in fearless decision making, because you will find yourself making more right decisions.

MAKE SMALL DECISIONS PROMPTLY

Urgency often decides for you the way you go about making your decision. You just do not always have the time to probe a problem in depth. Making a "federal case" out of every little problem is enough to scare anyone away from decision making. You can take much of the fear out of decision making simply by knowing what must be done *now* and what can safely wait.

Many times you will find that on-the-spot counseling, a quick search through your files, maybe just a telephone call is all you need to make some decisions wisely as well as quickly.

Proscrastination is not only an obstacle to efficiency, it is also generally regarded as a symptom of fear to make decisions! Don't, however, confuse procrastination with prudent restraint—when you do not have all the facts, or are prevented by diplomatic or other strong reasons from acting positively. "Strategic Hesitation" is the inspired way Mr. F. E. Rickel, Director of Marketing, Steel City Division, Midland-Ross Corporation, terms the cautious handling of a tricky situation.

As a spur to speedier decision making, the executives of Honeywell, Inc. have ever before them this query from their founder, Mr. W. R. Sweatt: "Shall we do this definitely, clearly, sincerely, energetically and above all, *immediately*, or shall we continue to drift and talk?"

LET OTHERS HELP YOU

Doing everything yourself can also give your superiors the idea that you are afraid to make decisions.

Leonard Carr, time expert for the Swift Freight Company knew more about the organization than anyone except its owner. Leonard appeared qualified to climb the executive ladder. He may have, too, if he had ever stood still long enough for anybody to talk to him about it.

Everybody at the Swift Freight Company knew that if you wanted to get Leonard's ear, you had to "set a trap" for him such as pouncing on him in the washroom or even blocking his way as he rushed incessantly and anxiously about.

Leonard stayed so busy that he didn't always get to the conferences or monthly luncheons of the company executives. When asked why, his usual reply was, "I'm afraid to leave anyone else in charge. If I want anything done right around here, I have to do it myself."

Thus, Leonard hoped to make himself indispensable to the organization, but it had the unfortunate effect of causing management to take a dim view of his decision-making ability. The promotions invariably went to others.

The "easy" way is often the smarter and the more efficient method of getting things done. Give yourself time for right decision making with "executive savers" like these:

1. Utilize fully other departments best equipped to handle certain operations, mailing, duplicating, etc.
2. Show your secretary how to manage routine correspondence, including phone calls. She can also make your travel and hotel reservations, file, receive some of your callers, etc.
3. Become proficient in the use of tape recorders.
4. Use form letters and other prepared aids.
5. When traveling keep pad and pencil handy for "brainwaves" as they occur to you.
6. Confer, advise, and orient during "off" hours whenever possible.
7. Cut down size of gatherings to minimum—invite only those immediately concerned. ("Honorary" guests take more time, make more work.)

Divide Your Work into Two Parts

What your subordinates can do.
What only you can do.

In a large group, let the more competent or "key" individuals direct the others. Teach your subordinates to walk on their own feet with a minimum of guidance from you. Show your ability and fearlessness to make decisions by concentrating on the most important factors and delegating to competent assistants those tasks which they can and should handle.

WHEN TO SAY "NO"

Popularity gives you a great feeling, but being a "good old Joe" can be a burden and a time waster. Good old Joes often find themselves doing things they wish they weren't.

Say "no" to those unwarranted requests for help and to those invitations (however appealing) that end up wasting your time. When you have to stay after others have left for the day, it is small comfort to remember how the gang enjoyed your company during that extra coffee break.

Add a dash of restraint to straight thinking and your "no's" can become important, right decisions of far-reaching, desirable consequences.

Welcome Responsibility

What you think is timidity to make decisions may actually be just fear to assume responsibility for your actions. You have to fight such an apprehension, because decision making is practically synonymous with acceptance of responsibility. Any attempt to sever the two is impossible.

I have a friend on the New York City police force who is still in the ranks although he is unusually intelligent, industrious, and holds several degrees. His refusal to move up into the managerial level stems from only one source: he is reluctant to take on more responsibility. He once confided that he just could not face up to the possibility of having to "answer for" a subordinate at Headquarters, if an important document should be misplaced or some other similar "catastrophe" should occur.

Leadership, decision making, and responsibility are permanently joined together. The ambitious executive not only cannot be afraid of responsibility, he must welcome it. Your responsibility includes an obligation both to work for the successful completion of an assignment and to accept the blame wherever merited for errors made by you or your subordinates. If you need a "scapegoat" when things go wrong, you are not ready to lead.

Take the fear out of being responsible by taking advantage of sheltered responsibility to develop your decision-making know-how!

Under the protective canopy of your superior's responsibility for your actions, you can "painlessly" profit from your mistakes—providing you don't blunder too often! Think of it like swimming in a sheltered cove—if you stick your neck out too far, your boss should be able to pull it back in.

Four men assigned to a complicated operation were receiving the necessary instructions. In the middle of the session the boss was needed in another location. "Sorry, I can't show you the rest of it now, boys. It will have to wait until tomorrow." "Boss," said one of the men, "I've seen a similar operation, may I try to explain it?" The supervisor barely hesitated before replying, "OK, I know you're a capable guy. Go ahead. I'll be back in time to handle any questions that you can't answer."

The job was well done under the volunteer's guidance, and this turned out to be just the beginning for our intrepid friend who went far—fast.

The "good man in a pinch" moves on up. Management is ever on the lookout for *key men* to fill supervisory openings. They are looking for people who can handle others, carry out orders and *make decisions*. You develop decision-making know-how when you:

> *Volunteer for responsibility.*
> *Listen* carefully to instructions, then *act on your own*, without running to your superior for constant guidance.
> *See every assignment through.*

Master the Techniques of Problem Solving

Some problems are so involved and affect so many people that they must be approached with the utmost caution. At these times, arriving at the best solution can take a long time and be very costly. However, like an intricate dance which is but an elaborate combination of certain routine steps, so too are all problems, both large and small, solved by the same fundamental techniques. The more complicated problems just take longer, that's all.

Open the door to fearless decision making with these four golden keys to problem solving:

1. Identify the Problem.
2. Find the Causes.
3. Weigh the Possible Inferences.
4. Decide on the Best Solution.

WHAT IS THE PROBLEM?

Which is the problem and which are the symptoms are not always immediately apparent, and this is where an analytical approach is indispensable. Be suspicious of the too easy or too agreeable (to you) solution.

What sometimes appears to be a series of problems, for instance, may only be one problem with a series of attendant, unfortunate events.

This was the case in one plant where a department was afflicted with absenteeism, loafing, griping and, of course, low productivity. At first these cases were dealt with individually to no apparent benefit. Finally, but not without considerable cost in time, money and effort, someone on the staff noticed that the workers in this group were struggling to meet quotas virtually impossible with the out-dated equipment on hand.

Think Straight. Start by writing down everything you know about the situation as it occurs to you or is brought to your attention. When you have finished listing all you know, rearrange the data into its proper or logical sequence. Seeing it all down in black and white before you should enable you to pick out the most important items. The proper identification of the problem is a prerequisite to determination of the solution.

What Caused the Problem?

Ferreting out the real cause or causes of a problem will usually indicate the possible soultions as well. To find out *why* the problem:

> Investigate
> Compare
> Deduce

Talk to All Concerned, but beware of acting upon mere hearsay. Look for the answers to What, When, Where, How, and Why.

A problem is sometimes so wedded to other problems that it seems to be indivisible from the others, as in this case brought before a union employee counselor.

Luis Caldos had been termed a "problem" worker. At the time of his hiring Luis appeared to be qualified for the job in question. His work background, while not impressive, was adequate. Why then was Luis not measuring up?

Was it because he could not or would not follow instructions since he ethnically did not "fit in" with the rest of the work group? Or was it because his wife had just run off with another man?

Actually, all of these factors were large contributors to the worker's inability to perform satisfactorily. It was impossible to give Luis any significant help by trying to isolate and treat a single cause.

By examining all the data in the context of the whole, it was possible to pinpoint the crucial area of difficulty directly related to the man's unsatisfactory performance.

Luis could not adequately carry out instructions for a very simple, basic reason: he understood very little English! Ethnically then he was not a "member of the team."

Learning to speak English would not necessarily solve the problem, because the other mentioned factors could still continue to adversely influence this worker's behavior, but it was the correct *first* step, because if not corrected the language barrier would always prevent Luis from performing productively and being accepted by his work group.

Visualize a Problem in Its Entirety, then separate it into workable components. You do this through the process of *analysis* and *synthesis.*

Analysis consists of separating the whole into all of its parts and studying each part.

Synthesis is the process of learning the nature of the whole through an analysis of the component parts, or the reverse procedure of analysis.

What Are the Possible Inferences?

In the absence of necessary information, you have to guess. Cut down the risk here by learning how to make "educated" guesses. These are the result of thorough job knowledge, experience and sharp observation.

You can make a good "guess" about which workers you can rely on in a crisis by noting from day to day how each reacts to pressures of the job. You can also note the natural leader, and who is willing to assume responsibility.

This is is not the same as jumping to conclusions like the traveler who late one night had a flat tire on a lonesome country road and discovered he did not have a jack in the trunk of his car.

Perceiving an unlighted farmhouse some distance away, he set out for it to seek assistance. On the way he began to ponder what his own reaction would be, if he were the awakened farmer asked to lend his jack to an intruder. By the time he arrived at the front door, the traveler was so worked up by his reflections and fears generated by the barking dogs, that when the hapless farmer opened his door, he was instantly floored by a punch in the nose. "Who needs your old jack anyway?" was the traveler's parting shot to the horizontal farmer who had never said a word.

What is true (a fact) and what is not true are sometimes hard to distinguish. In this area you must fight your natural inclination to believe what you want to believe or to make up your mind before you know what the facts are.

Rationalization is the opposite of logical thinking. It is an attempt to justify what you have already made up your mind to do, despite the facts, as well as the unconscious (or deliberate) interpretation of the facts to fit your preconceived ideas. Then again, you are rationalizing when you only look for those facts which indicate a course you desire.

Because the logical person can recognize a fact, appraise it accurately, and draw the right conclusion, he makes better decisions with less fear.

What Is the Best Solution?

We all envy the person who does the right thing by "intuition." Yes, "playing your hunches" does sometimes produce the desired results, and anyone can cite a corroborating example or two. If, however, you examine closely enough these gifted few who seem to have a "feeling" for the right actions at the right times, more than likely you will find that these individuals are preconditioned to these desirable impulses by habits of logical thinking and deductions.

Most of us, however, must rely on accurate information to make the proper decisions. This is not to say that you cannot make a good decision with incomplete facts. Indeed many decisions must be made this way because of the unavailability or the expense in time and money that might be required to obtain all missing information. Nevertheless, you should know what facts are missing, so that there will be awareness of the risks involved in taking the indicated action.

The best solution to a problem can be, but seldom is, the most obvious one. Sometimes, despite the amount and accuracy of your information, the solution remains tantalizingly elusive. It is better at such times to walk away from the problem for a while before you let frustration and emotion lead you into acting in a hasty or biased manner.

Your trouble could be unwillingness to act on the facts. Besides being hard to find, the best solution can also be one you do not like and are unconsciously resisting for that very reason.

Mr. H. H. Watson, formerly an executive with General Electric Company, like all leaders, had to make some decisions he did not like. Perhaps the most reluctant decision he ever made was to discharge a man he personally liked, for the good of the company. "No amount of sweetening," declares Hank, "either in the form of counseling or trying to relocate the misfit ever completely obliterated the bad taste this episode left." The whole unpleasant situation was made even more so by the pleading of the worker's wife who personally tried to dissuade Hank from the stand he had to take. Convinced that his decision was best for the company, Hank did not relent, but being a nice guy, he felt terrible.

Such has been Hank's reputation for making right decisions, that today, although retired from the General Electric Company, his services are in even greater demand.

Weigh and evaluate the facts. Remember that the best solutions are:

> Economical.
> Efficient (workable and time saving).
> Fair.
> Based upon Facts.
> Meet Current Needs.
> Foresee Future Trends or Needs.

Right decisions not only take care of immediate needs, they are also readily adaptable to changing requirements. How your decision will affect other areas of the business—above, on the same level, and below—should be factored into the deliberations.

CAUTION: Reduce the risk in making an important decision, especially those involving other people, by consulting with your superiors or other competent advisors.

In all but very isolated cases, you have much help at your disposal for keeping up to date and arriving at the best solution. Take advantage of inspirational sources like specialized newsletters, trade associations, professional journals, computer and statistical services, management consultants and, of course, legal counsel.

At best, however, these aids counsel and inform. Do not count on them to identify *your* problem, tell you what to do nor to show you:

How to Make Your Decision Work

Many people can recognize a problem and make plans to resolve it. This is not executive know-how, unless you also have the capacity to put your plan to work and see it through to completion.

Effective actions are the result of:

Straight thinking.
Acceptance of Responsibility.
Initiative.
Persistence.

Your solution may look fine on paper, but will it work?

Mr. David McGonagle, Vice-President of the West Virginia Armature Company, tells how, after much consultation, a purchasing agent finally came up with an "ideal" solution to the vexing problem of the vanishing light bulbs.

Starting on a certain date, only those employees turning in a used bulb would be given a new one. To the purchasing agent's utter discomfiture, his follow-up records showed that the number of bulb replacements had soared astronomically after the start of the new policy. The workers were bringing burned-out bulbs from home!

You Have to Consider the Human Element. Your decision is no more effective than the people carrying it out. When decisions affect others (and they generally do), it is important that your objectives be compatible with theirs.

Have Faith in Your Decisions. Assuming you have used the preceding "Golden Keys" for solving your problem, you can now set the stage for the desired action by creating a "climate of success."

1. Select the Right People to Do the Task
2. Watch the Timing
3. Communicate Clearly
4. Follow Up

Create a "Climate of Success"

What do big companies do when they are about to launch a new product? They advertise. They make the new item attractive to the prospective buyers.

I could name many industry leaders who enjoy a "history of success" in the enthusiastic response to their ideas. Experience has taught their colleagues that these men's ideas *work*. Many of the recipients are unaware that views sought, discussions of theories, testing of attitudes and investigations underway are all part of their preconditioning for a proposal that may be months away.

Get behind the scene and set the right mood of acceptance by those who will carry out your directions. When making decisions that directly affect others (working hours, replacements, innovations, furnishings, salaries, etc.) talk to them about it beforehand. Their views before a decision can point you in the right direction.

One management thought about having a coffee wagon pass through the building once each morning and afternoon. In talking it over with some of his subordinates, the manager was surprised to find objection. To his astonishment, the workers thought the idea was a time waster and a form of regimentation. They expressed preference for a coffee dispensing machine, and so it was.

"My problem" confessed one plant owner to me, "is trying to convey something new to my workers. They're worse than my kids for resisting changes."

At Wilson Brothers Corporation, the employees are just as addicted to comfortable sameness as any other workers, but they cheerfully follow their leader wherever he leads them. Why?

Frank thinks it's because he and his brother, co-owner, "feel out" their workers' reactions before they make any innovations.

Recently, the brothers decided to try a new computerized service "guaranteed to promote greater efficiency," as the salesman glibly put it. The new system would entail considerable shifting of personnel in order to avoid discharging anyone. Some of these relocations would of necessity be slight demotions. How to do this without arousing ill will and resistance was the brothers' main concern.

Frank decided to throw the problem at his workers to test their reactions. He began by calling a meeting and explaining the new system, naturally emphasizing its more desirable features. In the touchy area of relocations, he carefully stressed the important training features of the new jobs. The workers were made to appreciate that they were "pioneers" in their community of an advanced, highly prophetic phase of their industry.

The meeting ended with workers volunteering to man the new positions. Frank and his brother actually had to "screen" the applicants.

Compare the approach of the Wilson Brothers to one of trying to force your decisions down the throat of your subordinate. The latter is almost guaranteed to foster resistance, an apathetic compliance or outright subversion of your projects.

It is a long time since the Saturday afternoon I had a date with a young friend to go to the movies. When I called for my pal, his father said he first had to plow the corn field. It would then be too late to go to the movies. I watched as the disgruntled youth recklessly and spitefully plowed under many dollars worth of his father's crop.

On that Saturday long ago I learned how true it is that "You can lead a horse to water, but you can't make him drink."

Select the Right People

Match your people to their tasks. You need the right people to carry out your instructions. Their proper selection can make the big difference between success or failure of your ideas. Do not, cautions Ed Shulenburg, President of Traffic Signal, Inc., give a worker responsibility above his capacity to perform adequately.

Know Whom You Can Depend On. In any important undertaking do not delegate authority to individuals who appear hesitant to assume responsibility. Your subordinates are sometimes very well aware of their own limitations and it is a mistake not to heed or at least take a careful look at such "stop signs."

The most competent helpers in the world cannot successfully put over your ideas if they are handicapped with faulty, outdated, or insufficient tools. Give your decisions every chance to work out, by providing your helpers with the necessary equipment to put them into effect.

WATCH THE TIMING

"Tomorrow may be too late" is no truer than "Today may be too soon." The good or bad outcome of your plans can just as easily hinge on the one as on the other.

Timing is often the most unpredictable catalyst in implementing your decisions. Remember that people laughed at Franklin, Ford and Einstein, because they were ahead of their time. More tears are shed, however, over what might have been than over what could be.

Usually your ideas are more likely to succeed if you "strike while the iron is hot." If you spend too much time waiting till everyone is in the "right mood" you may lose your chance to score.

COMMUNICATE CLEARLY

Does everyone involved thoroughly understand his role? Let each participant know how his operation fits into the whole picture.

Give detailed instructions in simple, easy to understand language—demonstrate if necessary.

Watch for Feedback. This can tip you off to something wrong before it is too late.

FOLLOW UP

Stay with your project until it is satisfactorily completed. In those instances where tasks are assigned to others, provide for reports so you can follow the status and be kept abreast of any problems as they arise.

Learn from Mistakes

Don't be afraid of mistakes. Profit from them.

In the hazardous realm of decision making, you can always count on "Murphy's Law":

"If anything can go wrong, it will."

"Nothing is as easy as it looks."

"It will take longer than you think."

No doubt about it, you will certainly make some mistakes. If you aspire to higher management levels, however, it is riskier to make no decision than to make the wrong one. Your biggest enemy of executive development is indecision.

The worst thing about mistakes is their cost in time and money to your company. The best thing about mistakes is what you learn from them. If nothing else, you can always fall back upon your "Vast Experience of Failures," as Mr. William V. White, Executive Director, National Commission on Product Safety, likes to put it.

Generally, it is not a good rule to admit to subordinates that you are wrong, except when a bad situation cannot be remedied, or unless others will be blamed for your mistake. If additional facts come to light indicating a different solution from the one you have directed, it is preferable to make an adjustment, rather than to completely revoke a prior decision. This avoids eroding the confidence of subordinates in your ability to make decisions that can stand.

Most important of all is not to dwell on past mistakes nor try to salvage the irreparable. Alibis are a waste of time, and you can't put toothpaste back into the squeezed tube. When you "lay an egg," you have no sensible alternative but to get rid of it as fast as you can.

Remember, to get angry about errors will usually cost you more time than doing something about it. Instead, put your time to good use by analyzing:

> What Went Wrong?
> How It Went Wrong?
> What You Can Do Now?

WHAT WENT WRONG?

Did you try to accomplish too much at once? "One thing at a time and that done well" is a good rule for any executive or would-be executive. Although you may know some "juggler" types of individuals who can do well various jobs at a time, it is a risky procedure.

Ask Yourself:

> Have I completely analyzed this problem?
> Did I mistake symptoms for the real problem?

Did I overlook any important detail?

Did I have enough facts?

Did I rely on hearsay rather than on facts?

Did I reject help from others?

Am I drawing unwarranted inferences?

Did I understand the motives, emotions, conflicts, of the interested parties?

Were there adequate communications?

Did I act on impulse?

Was I prejudiced or partial?

Did I overlook an important "gray" area?

An IBM Engineering Group had to decide:

1. Whether to use an existing electrical circuit which required a specific resistor thought to be in short supply,
   or
2. Redesign the circuit at a cost of approximately $6000, eliminating the particular resistor.

A check with the California office of IBM verified that the particular resistor was available, so the engineers decided to keep the existing circuit.

What was wrong with that decision? The wrong question was asked of the California office. The engineer learned only that the resistor was available (known all along), but not in the quantity needed by IBM.

COSTLY RESULT: IBM had to redesign the circuit with the added cost of production changeover and resulting delay.

How Did It Go Wrong?

Re-examine your objectives and methods of implementation. It's not always your fault when something goes wrong. There are misunderstandings, unavailability of vital information, or orders may not have been carried out. There may be quirks, and always unforeseen and unavoidable events that work against the best laid or thought-out plans.

Consider these cases:

1. An unprecedentedly warm spell one winter caused substantial losses in several department stores that suddenly

found themselves overstocked in heavy garments and other cold-weather accessories.

2. Vincent Trahey bought a piece of land with intent to construct an auto service center for prospective shoppers in the vicinity. The expected shopping center never materializes there, and Trahey was left "holding the bag."

3. A jet passenger plane crashed, and a major corporation is bereft of its entire sales staff.

In the case of the department stores, the buyers did not err in their estimates of their stores' cold season needs—the weather failed to cooperate. It might be years or never before that part of the country "enjoys" another mild winter. Still store managers' decisions must factor in the law of averages.

NEXT TIME: The buyers will be more cautious and hedge buy—probably erring on the conservative side. It can also be anticipated that caution will be exercised in other buying operations to avoid eroding the profits contemplated in the winter clothing sales.

In case 2, Mr. Trahey might be running a profitable auto service center today if, at the time of purchasing his land, he had known all the facts. He was afraid that someone else would think of his idea and grab up that piece of land. A thorough investigation would have revealed that the proposed new highway was being considered for the other side of town. Naturally, the new shopping center followed it.

NEXT TIME: Mr. Trahey will look before he pours his resources into a worthless hillside.

In case 3, you might call the crash of the jet airliner an "Act of God" that nobody could foretell or prevent. True enough, but it is often a company policy not to take such risks. It is a standard safeguard in many firms to require executives to travel on separate planes.

NEXT TIME: This firm will take precautions against unnecessary risks involving its personnel.

WHAT CAN YOU DO NOW?

You always have the alternative of doing nothing immediately, especially if you lack vital information. Even serious situations that dictate prompt action need not have instant solutions. Normally, however, corrections should be more prompt than the initial decision, because your earlier decision may already be working against the firm.

To help you decide whether to repair or discard an unsatisfactory situation, consider:

1. What other solutions are there?
2. Will the other solutions create new problems?

The answers to these questions will help you to: (a) get a true picture; (b) weigh one or more possible actions; (c) evaluate the possible consequences; and (d) make a better decision this time.

Now make the corrections or revisions dictated by your findings, if the project is worth saving. For instance, look for a suitable replacement if the cause of failure was the inability of the person to handle the task assigned.

Whatever you do, don't stay on a collision course. Willing it so never makes a wrong decision right. A closed mind is as fatal to good decision making as the trap door under the hangman's noose.

A friend living in the Boston area described one candidate for mayor of that city as a person with a "trap door" mind.

In the face of repeated and unmistakable evidence that a very unpopular platform was being expounded, the candidate refused to give an inch—and lost the election.

NEXT TIME: Be prepared for the worst! Have a spare or an alternative solution—in case of an emergency.

There are such means as trial balloons and polls for risky decisions. I once had a shrewd boss who seemed always to be shifting the people around for improvement in performance. Before each shift was made, he "accidentally" left his sketch of new seating locations on his desk, and listened for the back play.

Finally, there are those fateful times when you will be "damned" if you do and "damned" if you don't. In such crises your best ally is good old-fashioned integrity. Don't be afraid to do what *you* feel is morally right. Then come what may, you still have your self-respect—a most satisfying souvenir.

Review

One right decision may open the door of success to you, but you need a habit of making right decisions to move up the ladder of success in business.

Everyone makes mistakes. Neither blow them up nor ignore them. Learn from them. They are even blessings in disguise—if they teach you to stop, look and listen before they grow into worse disasters.

Overcome the fear of making mistakes by learning to correctly analyze the problem, the people, the facilities, the difficulties, (both apparent and hidden), and to predict future needs.

Many solutions that should be obvious remain hopelessly obscure when you look for the solution before the problem is analyzed.

Good decisions are the result of straight thinking. The main characteristic of straight thinking is *order*.

Thinking through a difficult problem is the logical way to go about its solution.

Logic is often just another way of saying common sense. For example, it is just plain common sense (hence logical) to:

Look before you leap.

Rely on facts rather than on hearsay.

Discount emotional influences (prejudice, favoritism, and personal desires).

Act on facts.

Decision-making fears have a way of dissolving when you use an orderly approach.

Nothing succeeds like success. The sure way to take the fear out of decision making is to build a series of successful decisions—first little ones, then the bigger ones come easy.

CHAPTER SIX

Develop the Knack of
Effective Supervision

John Smith of the ABC Products, Inc. runs a "tight ship"—his subordinates are an orderly, efficient and productive group. On the other hand, Warner B. Henderson of AAA Manufacturing Corporation guides his team with a loose rein. The results are equally good.

So, if you are looking for a surefire formula, there is no single one. What makes both formulas work? The magic ingredient is *compatibility*. By compatibility I do not necessarily mean that you and your subordinates have to "take to each other." It means that your control methods fit the needs of your helpers.

Study your subordinates—some workers want and need direct supervision. They can only perform satisfactorily when summarily commanded to "do this," or "do that." Others show a high degree of initiative, doing their best when given a voice in their activities.

The degree of compatibility between you and your subordinates directly affects (for better or worse) the quality of their performance, their attitude, morale and even the amount of satisfaction they derive from their work. Your incentive to yield a noteworthy performance is higher than that of your subordinates. It won't always be easy to convince them that the overall goal is worthwhile and beneficial to them as well as to the company. Proclamations and edicts issued incompatible with the needs of your workers are not likely to produce positive results.

Cause and effect are very important in supervision. See how they

117

were inseparable in the case of a large manufacturing firm that was showing an alarmingly consistent loss over a period of several months. The owners finally conferred with management consultants who recommended certain changes in one of the operations. After the suggestions were followed the company still continued to operate in the red.

Why? Further examination revealed that the supervisor in charge of the new phase did not (or could not) adequately instruct the workers in the proper innovations, and they had slipped back to the old ways.

Whether you supervise one or many, your underlying objective remains the same, namely, to direct your subordinates' efforts toward achieving your company's goals most efficiently and with the least friction. Executive know-how is more important than straight order-giving in establishing a supervision policy compatible with company aims and the leadership needs of your subordinates.

You are *not* in control when your workers show:

> Lack of cooperation
> Lack of enthusiasm
> Lack of discipline
> Low quality performance and poor production
> Low morale and resulting gripes
> High employment turnover
> Poor business manners
> Inadequate communications
> Refusal to accept criticism without blaming someone else.

Know Your Subordinates

You can see right away that the same yardstick will not be adequate for all workers. However, because people are much more like each other than they are unlike, you can lean confidently on these ten guides to effective supervision:

1. Have Thorough Job Knowledge
2. Recognize That Your Authority Is Limited
3. Respect Workers' Rights
4. Plan and Schedule Work Efficiently
5. Delegate Responsibility to Capable Subordinates
6. Develop Group Incentive

7. Set the Pace
8. Stick Up for Your Subordinates
9. Follow Up Without Snooping
10. Keep Continuing Records of Performance

Have Thorough Job Knowledge

If you don't know the policies and functions of your company, you cannot assemble an effective work unit. Do you know your organization's product, policies and place in the business world? Are you familiar with the responsibilities of each management level, and are you able to visualize the overall structure? Concentrating on just one limited area hinders your executive growth—sometimes stops it cold.

Start now to learn as much as possible about the workings of your organization so that you can effectively evaluate the relative merits and duties of your subordinates. Use your company library. Enroll in business courses. Don't overlook outside information—at least review technical publications associated with your industry, and keep abreast of advances in the markets served by your company.

Recognize That Your Authority Is Limited

Any power associated with your status belongs to the position and not to you as a person. You do not have authority over others in the business area; you are merely allowed to use specific, recognized tools and procedures to achieve the desired performance.

A little humility helps you to work out a compatible arrangement with your subordinates. Try putting yourself in their place. How would you react in a similar situation? Seniority over subordinates in years of employment and age helps them to accept your authority more readily. Lacking this crutch, you have to try harder to win their respect and following.

Do you know the limitations on your range of authority? Everett Williston, a beginning junior executive, did not. Very proud of his newly achieved authority, he couldn't wait to exercise it. When his subordinate asked to change his lunch hour to coincide with that of a friend, Everett instantly obliged.

The new arrangement proceeded satisfactorily until Mr. Williston's superior, the Department Manager, noticed Everett's assistant wasting time during the regular lunch hour. The Manager made some pointed comments on the spot. Much to Everett's embarrassment, a memo was also issued instructing all in the department to observe the same lunch hour.

MORAL: Always "clear the decks" with your superior lest he countermand your decisions.

RESPECT WORKERS' RIGHTS

Every worker is entitled to a full measure of *justice*. Injustice lowers morale, generates gripes and unfriendliness, and is often at the root of high employee turnover. Your subordinates should bask in some of the glory for accomplishing the objectives.

Do you practice courtesy without familiarity?

Do you protect the dignity of your workers and make an unbiased appraisal of their worth to the organization?

In a poll taken of factory workers over a large cross section of the country, favoritism was listed as the injustice most resented by employees. Workers expect to be reprimanded when they are not performing up to par, just as they expect some sign of recognition and encouragement for a task especially well done.

Mr. J. E. Wilson of the Parker Brothers Corporation rose from the ranks to general foreman. At first, neither he nor his people felt that he favored former friends, but gradually Joe began "jumping" on a man for an infraction, and overlooking it in one of his buddies. He was a tyrant with some and moderate with others.

Within a relatively short time the less favored workers developed open hostility toward those who "stood in with the boss." There was a lowering of group morale and output. Joe Wilson had to be replaced before he learned that *fairness helps win respect*.

PLAN AND SCHEDULE WORK EFFICIENTLY

A necessary function of supervising is the planning and scheduling of work—your own and that of others. This calls for ability to define the problem and to take into account both the ordinary and the unusual. Successful planning will provide you with a yardstick for measuring accomplishment.

Here are five ways to plan an effective work schedule:

1. Collect all information available on the specific activity.
2. Break the job down into parts.

3. Determine which functions are the most important, and program them in a logical sequence.
4. Figure out the amount of time needed for each one and see that everyone follows the schedule. Some operations (the baking industry for example) call for split-second timing.
5. Factor in down time, set-ups, time off, training, etc.

Efficiency is completing a job in the shortest time possible and with the least expenditure of energy and resources. Successful allocation of time and energy begins with the establishment of a priority system. What is most important? Have your assistants tackle the most difficult assignments first (when other factors are equal).

In all dealings with people, be prepared for a certain amount of frustration arising out of delays, interruptions, inefficiency, etc. Expect problems, but don't waste time with worry.

Devise a workable time schedule like this:

1. Keep careful records of activities over a period of time.
2. Group your assignments according to the individuals who will carry them out.
3. Pinpoint the most important duties and give them preference. (Allocation of time for more routine duties will naturally follow.)

Where work details are complex, it helps to write them down. Preferably, arrange them to serve as effective instructions. A compatible (effective) team is your reward if you first:

1. Prepare subordinates *who* are to receive your instructions, including *what* is to be accomplished.
2. Outline the procedure, calling attention to the major points, including *why* it is being done.
3. Have the employee perform the job under observation, after *how* has been demonstrated.
4. Inform *when* the task is to be performed.
5. Place the worker on the job *where* the job is to be performed, and check his operation, re-explaining the details.
6. Assign the task in such a manner that it will not overwhelm the worker. (Break it up into small segments.)
7. Make assignments in recognition of the limitations of the

worker's ability. (Also restrictions of the job and tools provided.)

You get better results when:

The worker is fitted to the job (job knowledge, health, and ability to comprehend).

Duties and responsibilities are clearly defined.

Directions are clearly set forth.

The quantity and quality of work desired are emphasized.

Don't just hope or pray that workers will perform satisfactorily like Coley L. King, a part-time minister in South Carolina who was appointed supervisor in a local textile plant. The owners expected great things of Coley, who was a dynamic preacher with an enthusiastic following. Aware of this, Coley worried when the production of his department did not rise dramatically under his direction. Unlike his Sunday congregation, Coley's subordinates were woefully unresponsive to him. He was using his fire and brimstone tactics that had won him fame in the pulpit. What had happened to his old magic?

Frustrated, he turned to his source of spiritual strength and prayed to God to make his workers perform as they should. In vain, Coley looked for the answer to his prayers in terms of changes in his subordinates, and the harder he prayed, the more subjective he became. In time, Coley lost both his congregation and his job without ever recognizing the incompatibility of his preaching technique with the supervisory needs of his subordinates.

Custom fit your production requirements to the abilities and limitations of your subordinates and equipment.

DELEGATE RESPONSIBILITY TO CAPABLE SUBORDINATES

Are you mistrustful of your subordinates and convinced that at all times they must be rigidly controlled and directed? Ask any group of executives how they feel about delegating authority to subordinates, and nine out of ten will tell you it is the only way to get the job done where your responsibilities exceed your physical capacity to perform them.

In practice, however, almost as many of them mete out authority to subordinates grudgingly, and then only as little as possible. In holding a worker accountable for results without delegating commensurate authority, you deprive him of a strong motivator as well as a highly satisfactory compensation.

Of course, the trick of successfully delegating responsibility to subordinates is *to know which workers you can count on*. Careful observation will soon reveal which of your assistants are natural "lead men." Here's how to ferret them out. Look for:

> Who commands the respect of the other workers?
> Who leads?
> Who are the self-starters?
> Who really understands the job that must be done?
> Who can handle minor conflicts without running to you for guidance?

Once a choice is made, assign responsibility only after you decide what aspects of the assignment you must handle yourself and which ones will be delegated. Whenever you cannot assign appropriate authority, clearly define the line of delegation, but let the subordinate choose his own assistants from among the work group. After responsibility and authority have been established, plan for subsequent follow-up without meddling.

You establish compatibility when you do not countermand the actions of a subordinate in the area for which he is responsible. If there are complaints, conflicts, questions, etc., submitted to you over his head, either refer them to the responsible subordinate, or at most only agree to look into the matter.

Mr. Charles Marten, Personnel Director of Harley Enterprises, had appointed a foreman to supervise a certain project involving several workers. The new supervisor noticed that one of his assistants, Bill Adams, consistently absented himself from the job for long intervals at a time. Unable to obtain a satisfactory explanation from the rather surly recalcitrant, he suspended him for a week, whereupon the offended worker appealed to Mr. Marten and demanded to be reinstated at once.

Although Mr. Marten did not see eye to eye with his young assistant's disciplinary measure, he did not let the aggrieved worker know this, allowing the decision to stand. Having no satisfactory alternative, the worker waited out his suspension and returned with a new, if grudging, respect for his young supervisor, which carried over to the rest of the work group.

WORTH REMEMBERING: You are never absolved from ultimate accountability.

It Is Not Easier to Do It Yourself

Harry Jenkins had supervised the same manufacturing operation for many years. No one knew the different functions better than he. The trouble was he believed he was the only one who could do anything right, and he ran himself ragged overseeing and performing one job after another. Being indispensable was a source of great inner satisfaction to him, but he worked himself into early retirement.

When his successor took over, he was cautioned to follow in Jenkins' footsteps or the whole operation would fall apart. The new man, however, had other views. When the pressure would mount and it looked as if they were going to be snowed under, he would call the workers into his office for a conference. Helpful suggestions were solicited and wherever feasible were tried out.

Responsibility for getting the job done was spread out among all. Every man knew his role and that it was important to the overall objective. The supervisor was then free to answer questions and meet new challenges as they arose. Today he is one of the company's leaders.

DEVELOP GROUP INCENTIVE

Most of us have a desire to please and perform well when we see it as a means of being one of the team. During the Second World War, it was an Army technique to punish the conforming and allow the disobedient non-conformist to go "Scot Free" (on the assumption that his comrades would take corrective measures). While not exactly fair play, it did achieve the desired results. Of course, this is not a disciplinary measure adaptable to employee supervision, but you can control mavericks and non-conformists through their basic desire to belong.

When it appears that a subordinate just won't be motivated with reasonable inducements, remember that:

1. Only the mentally ill enjoy being parasites.
2. Most people begin the day with an earnest desire to do a good job, and it is often the things which happen after he awakens that prevent the fulfillment of this wish.

3. A healthy work climate helps immeasurably in developing a well-rounded employee and creates a willingness to co-operate in the accomplishment of the overall objectives of the firm.

Factor Reasonableness into Fairness. Whenever possible, avoid the use of expediency, especially in giving recognition, promotion and due credit. Workers who show advancement potential should be encouraged, without being singled out for promotions before they are ready. Side-step situations which can generate jealousy and antagonism among your workers.

Promote Cooperation. It will assure the success of your project. Just as you cannot be a little bit honest, neither can you be just a little bit cooperative. A person may, however, be cooperative in one task but not in another. Be tolerant of a worker's objectionable personality traits when they are unrelated to the project to be ac-complished.

Exercise a high degree of self-control in the following six areas:

1. The Ready Alibi
2. Jealousy
3. Domineering Attitude
4. Keeping Your Word
5. Egoism
6. Empire Building

Don't forget that the tone or manner in which you give an order can materially affect the spirit in which it will be accepted and executed. *Praise* is frequently a greater incentive for cooperation than more pay.

How do you create a cooperative, productive work unit? The more common ways are to:

Rotate jobs to relieve monotony.
Stress individual job importance.
Spur competition by setting hard, but not impossible, goals.
Foster pride in achievement by recognition and other forms of compensation.
Make workers quality conscious.
Show concern for worker safety and well-being.
Build a "You can do it" self-confidence.

There are almost as many methods of developing group incentive as there are work areas. I know one supervisor who makes a contest out of tedious jobs by offering a small prize to the one who finishes first. An associate of mine has had excellent results pitting competitive subordinates against one another, and I have had success in selling workers that "What is good for the organization is good for you."

Make the spirit of cooperation pervade the entire work environment—each worker a link in the overall chain. Every job, however small or menial, is important or it should not exist.

Put aside your pet theories, and use the suggestions of your helpers when they will accomplish the same objective just as efficiently.

Listen and Learn. Mr. R. L. Easley recalls a textile plant experience when he was supervising a thread spinning department. The "doffer" couldn't keep the yarn on top of the spinning frames, cutting down total production and adding to the work burden because yarn was used up so fast.

A spinner observed one day that if there were larger spools to hold the yarn they would not have to be replaced as often. This was the solution for speeding up the spinning of thread with less effort required by each worker.

Eliciting the cooperation of others includes the capacity to teach and inspire as well as to motivate them to perform in the desired manner. Your subordinates will cooperate best when they thoroughly understand the issues, so keep them informed on all matters that affect them.

Set the Pace

Workers follow the leader. Set a good example by getting to work on time and putting in a full day's effort with energy and goodwill even on days when you are not feeling your best. Lend a hand when your subordinates are experiencing difficulty in starting. *Your own enthusiasm for the task at hand is the single most motivating factor* for firing the zeal of your assistants.

Young Alex Stevenson was usually the last to show up and the first to leave. He could not understand why his office assistants were incurable clock watchers. They were always ten minutes ahead of lunch hours, coffee breaks and dismissal, but never put in an extra minute. Alex spent much time bemoaning his "bad luck," and envying the other executives whose staff diligently put in a whole day's productive work.

When you supervise a dangerous operation, it is important that you show the way in observing all safety rules. A foreman in a chemical plant was indirectly responsible for one of his men being severely burned. He never wore the prescribed safety equipment when overseeing his men, and the injured man did not believe he had to either. Do not just show how to do a job safely—*insist upon it.*

Set a pace which allows your helpers to keep up.

STICK UP FOR YOUR SUBORDINATES

Your subordinates rightfully expect you to back them up in disagreements or misunderstandings with other heads and co-workers. The loyalty of your subordinates is your reward for doing unto them as you would have your superiors do to you.

A worker's self-respect is one of his most valued rights. *Never allow others to criticize or reprimand those directly responsible to you.* Always correct in private.

You don't have to be the guardian angel of your subordinates, but under no circumstances let one of them become a "fall guy" or "goat" for mistakes arising from your failure to give adequate instructions. Accept the responsibility for the actions of all your subordinates, but without shielding them from constructive guidance.

Lend a sympathetic ear to your assistants, but when confidences reveal facts that could be damaging to the company, bring them to your superior's attention.

As a young executive, I once entrapped myself with a confidence from my secretary. While I was on a business trip my superior became annoyed with her, and personally reprimanded her. Later, swearing me to secrecy, she confided that because of his criticism she was going to leave the company.

At job appraisal time I learned that she was among the few to be granted an increase, and sought a release from her confidence. "No," she said, she was entitled to her raise while she sought a job elsewhere.

She took the raise and very soon thereafter left the company, but

I always felt guilty for not notifying my superior beforehand. Had I not accepted her confidence, the question of proper allegiance would never have come up.

FOLLOW UP WITHOUT SNOOPING

Follow-up or performance measurement is a vital aspect of effective supervision and control. Generally you will have specific standards or quotas to check against. This process of checking and rechecking helps you to compare how things are with how they they should be.

Whenever you find performance below standard, it pays to ask yourself:

1. Did I set unrealistic goals?
2. Do I have a correct report?
3. Is the worker properly fitted to the job?

Very often the success or failure of a project is directly related to how consistently you follow up the activities and listen for feedback. An on and off follow-up policy lowers group efficiency. Careful (but unobtrusive) checking at every phase notably cuts down costly mistakes which can result in delays, maladjustments, and low output.

Be on the lookout for unmeasurable factors. To accurately size up the situation, you need to know the temperaments and capabilities of your assistants and to draw the correct inferences. Watch out for behavior indicating low morale; stand ready to hear all problems. In other words, stay on top of the situation at all times.

Listening and Watching Pay. My father once supervised a mill hand who was capable of performing outstandingly at times, but occasionally did a very poor job. One morning my father overheard a conversation between the man and one of his co-workers. He was telling how years ago when he first started working he had hurt his back lifting heavy bales of cotton and had been laid up for weeks. My father started watching him and soon noticed that whenever his job called for lifting or stretching he walked away from the scene and absented himself until someone else had done the job. When my father found him a place where no lifting was involved, he became a reliable employee.

Your company's profits are of vital concern. A close follow-up of operations can uncover money losers like waste or inefficiency caused by not fitting the workers to the job. A factory specializing in low cost items for a mail order house was suffering from materials waste and failure to operate equipment to full capacity.

After taking note of the operations for a week, the supervisor tightened up the quality standards and delegated one of the workers to keep a close inspection on the others. He also made a few strategic personnel shifts and was shortly rewarded by increased yield, fewer defects, and lower production costs which further resulted in a handsome bonus for each worker at the end of the year.

KEEP CONTINUING RECORDS OF PERFORMANCE

Record keeping is the principal (and most effective) method of staying abreast of the activities you control, but don't drown yourself in a sea of data. Record only related or pertinent information. Know the job each of your subordinates is performing, the degree of individual responsibility, complexity of duties, working conditions, how long it takes him or her to "catch on," etc. Different companies use varying scales to measure output and performance. Among many others job and performance evaluations generally include the following, with appropriate values or points for each:

Production Quality	Leadership Know-How
Quantity of Yield	Intelligence
Initiative	Attendance
Health	Work Habits
Safety	Job Capacity
Dependability	Utilization of Materials

One manager I know runs a department envied for its efficiency. He is a regular tyrant about keeping records. His workers must report amount of materials used, number of hours spent on each job, etc. He comes down with a heavy hand on all non-conformists —even going so far as to call them at home when they forget!

Too strong? Fair as well as strict, this manager obtains a high degree of cooperation from his assistants. The real "method in his madness" is that he gets his workers to do much of the necessary record keeping for him, thus enabling him to spend more time in organizing and supervising his department.

See how consistent record keeping helped this company: A supervisor in charge of twenty men making replacement parts for mining equipment kept track of rejects over a period of time. He found that approximately eighty-eight out of each one hundred parts were satisfactory. Then he introduced the new ZD (Zero Defects) program, and the rejects have been reduced to a negligible percentage.

This was accomplished mainly by posting a daily performance review so that each worker was continually aware of his progress or lack of it. This also greatly facilitated the supervisor's record keeping and output evaluation. Multiplied many times over, the savings in unit production amounted to thousands of dollars annually.

Review

Any executive function will relate to one of these: *organize, delegate* or *supervise*. Knowing your subordinates will enable you to effectively combine all three into a compatible work program. Plan and schedule the work with due allocation of time and energy (your own and that of your assistants). Fit your supervision methods to the special requirements.

You can best adapt your workers to their job if you have a thorough knowledge of the necessary operations and are acquainted with the capabilities and weaknesses of your subordinates. Train your workers thoroughly in the techniques, equipment and safety measures of each job.

In a complex undertaking involving many people, portion out *appropriate responsibility and authority* to others to facilitate achieving your goal. Look for and select "lead" men, plainly spelling out the line of delegation to avoid misunderstandings. You retain complete responsibility for getting the job done, and are at all times accountable for your own actions and those of your subordinates.

Set the pace and maintain high morale among the work group, providing the necessary incentives for achieving wholehearted cooperation.

Keep your eyes and ears open for signs of apathy or discontent.

Earn the loyalty of your work team by standing ready to back them up and defend them.

Recognize the need to follow up and keep accurate continuing records of all operations and each worker's contribution. Set standards that can be measured and provide the necessary tools. Evaluate a worker's progress in terms and figures he can understand.

Keep your superior informed on your progress and problems.

Since not everything can be measured, you must use a human relations approach to search out the intangibles (attitudes, behavior, etc.) that define you as a leader, not a driver of men.

CHAPTER SEVEN

Use Positive Discipline for Better Results

You have to control your subordinates, or they will control you, but do not think of discipline as only a negative or punitive force. Punitive acts often have the negative side-effects of arousing resentment, lowering efficiency and blocking cooperation.

Forget about punishing and think in terms of *controlling* behavior. You get better results with positive discipline. There is more than one way to let your subordinates know that it pays to "play the game right."

Learn the Strategy of Subtle Discipline!

A clever supervisor knows that *rewards* are also a form of discipline. Know the strategic value of skillfully withholding favors as well as granting them. It is important to stress "skillfully."

The manager of a supermarket had announced that the store would be closed on the third Saturday of that month, providing a welcome and unexpected long weekend for the employees. In the interim, he noticed that some of the workers were leaving before quitting time, so he decided to teach them a lesson. He withdrew the promised holiday and made everybody come in that day to make up for the time lost by a few.

His unfair, unskilled handling of his subordinates boomeranged in sullen behavior and a high rate of employee turnover. The strategy of subtle discipline consists of *distinguishing between the contributions of subordinates.*

133

FAIRNESS NEED NOT MEAN EQUALITY

Consistency does not mean that you must deal identically with each subordinate. For example, you may refuse one worker's request for time off and give it to another, depending upon his or her degree of satisfactory performance. This would be fair but not equal treatment.

But, if you favor some workers more than others for personal reasons disassociated from their performance, you are unfair, and also inconsistent.

Note the negative results of always equating fairness with equality:

When large orders came in to Melvin Neuman's department, necessitating overtime work, he meted out the extra assignments with mathematical precision. Constant checking of his records reassured him that all workers were being treated alike. The fact that Nancy wanted to earn extra money for her trousseau, and that Grace didn't want to work overtime because she couldn't find a baby sitter meant nothing to Melvin.

Seething under Melvin's inflexibility, the girls soon had the manager on the spot. He was quite shaken to hear that he was being replaced for being so unfair.

TURN REFUSALS INTO EGO BOOSTERS

Subordinates tend to overestimate your capacity for dispensing favors. Junior executives are particularly restricted in their scope of authority, and all supervisors are limited by time and work schedules, nature of job, number of helpers, illness, accidents, etc. You may also have to refuse a worker's request because it is untimely or unseemly.

How then do you turn down requests without appearing to be stingy with your favors, or losing face? Be ready with alternate suggestions that not only save the day, but also serve as ego boosters for the subordinate's morale.

In the middle of a heavy work schedule, a good worker asked his superior for time off to check upon an advertised apartment out of town. Feeling he should grant this request, the supervisor first had the worker call to see if the apartment was still available and could be seen that day. The apartment had already been leased.

"What a close call," said the supervisor, "We were almost needlessly deprived of your valuable skills today. Don't you worry, I'll be on the lookout for you for another apartment." A satisfied worker returned to the job relieved that he had not gone out on a wild goose chase, and with that good feeling of being needed.

Compare this supervisor's executive know-how with young Frank Alvarez who granted a helper's request for an extra vacation day by swearing him to secrecy, and then asking him to call in sick. In making his subordinate lie, Alvarez lost that worker's respect and failed to reap a positive return for bestowing a favor.

Make Up Your Own Ego Boosters

In one company, the stenographic pool was made up of married women who worked on a temporary basis. They had agreed to only a half-hour lunch so they could leave that much earlier, but soon found it very hard to report back to work on time. Unable to grant their request for additional time, the supervisor instead set up a dining spot where her workers could eat their lunches brought from home.

Note how at the same time that she solved her workers' problem, she also made them feel she cared about their needs.

A timely sense of humor sometimes provides an unexpected ego booster:

During a shortage of skilled help, a manager had to retain an unsatisfactory (just this side of insubordinate) worker. He was giving her an assignment one day when an associate stopped by and asked, "How is everything going with you two?" "Great," said the knowing executive, "Peggy has decided to give me another chance." The ensuing laughter helped to dissolve the pent-up hard feelings the two had been harboring.

Similarly, your refusal to extend favors can subtly but positively convey to an unsatisfactory worker that it is to his advantage to improve performance.

Don't Be Afraid of Your Subordinates

Mr. Joe F. Ketzler, Chief Engineer of a large electrical plant, was once asked by a valued out-of-town client to make a hotel reservation for him in New York City. Sensing his client's concern about having a certain place to stay, Joe included in the instructions to his secretary the admonition to confirm the hotel reservation personally to the customer.

Thinking her boss a fuss-budget, the girl said, "Oh, let the hotel follow up; that is their job." Against his better judgment, but somewhat intimidated, Mr. Ketzler went along with her decision. The hotel management let them down, causing the client much discomfort, and placing upon Mr. Ketzler the burden of apologizing, reaffirming the reservation, and in other ways trying to placate his offended client.

Everybody makes mistakes, but it is not a remedy to let subordinates usurp your rightful authority to make decisions. Listen and learn from the suggestions of workers, but *you* make the decisions!

Don't try so hard to be "one of the boys" that you encourage strong-minded subordinates to intimidate or back you into a corner. Courteously, but firmly insist that your orders be carried out as issued.

It is not enough to know how to persuade your subordinates without antagonizing them, know also when to stand fast, and when to take corrective action.

Your ability to quietly convey an air of unmistakable control is a most subtle form of discipline that produces consistently positive results.

How to Cope with These Common Disciplinary Problems

It is getting harder all the time to fire unsatisfactory workers (the unions see to that), but discharge was never a cure-all for disciplinary problems. Can you be sure that you will be any luckier the next time around? A more positive technique is to convert the lax employee into a productive member of the work group.

Although disciplinary problems vary from company to company, and can be regional, occupational, or personal in nature, many personnel conflicts are recurring and common to all work environments. Their repetitiveness and general sameness have made it possible to derive much assurance of success through the use of certain standardized approaches to their solution. By no means exact formulas, these field tested techniques provide guidelines to effective control.

Learn how to deal positively with:

1. Lateness and Absenteeism
2. Abuse of Company Privileges

3. Non-Agression Pacts
4. Insubordination

LATENESS AND ABSENTEEISM

There are many good reasons why employees may be absent or late, but there is seldom justification for workers leaving before the appointed hour. The worker who habitually violates the prescribed working hours must be reoriented or disciplined for the sake of the general morale.

Reprimands had failed with Walter McHendricks who had a record of tardiness and absenteeism. He was highly skilled at justifying himself with hard to challenge excuses such as that he was ill, his wife or children were ill, accidents and other "emergencies."

WHAT WAS DONE

Walter's boss consulted with his own superior, and the next time that Walter asked for time off for a "dental appointment," he was ready for him. "What time," he asked, "are you expected, and how long will it take?" Thrown by this pointed querying, Walter had to think fast and hurriedly and replied, "Ten o'clock, and it will take about an hour."

"Fine," said his young supervisor, "then we'll expect you back on the job by 11:30." Feeling trapped, Walter returned to the job at the appointed time. As his boss continued to "call his bluff" Walter lost his taste for fabrication.

Some "ailing" absentees also experience instant "recovery" when directed to the plant physician, or asked to submit a medical report.

Eight Ways to Improve Attendance

1. Introduce special training in group orientation at the time the employee is hired.
2. Dramatize the importance of regular attendance by calling attention to those workers who have advanced or otherwise benefited by observing the rules and regulations.
3. Try "ego boosters" like praise and rewards for previous recalcitrants who show improvement.
4. Play up the need for each worker's presence on the job to lessen the job load of all.
5. Make each worker feel that he does his particular job best.

6. Pin down the habitual latecomer or absentee by asking him when, where, how and why.
7. Recognize every infraction even if only to comment, "Glad to have you back on the job," "What kept you," etc., depending upon the employee's record.
8. *Set a good example.*

ABUSE OF COMPANY PRIVILEGES

In the absence of management prescribed rules for desired employee behavior, you have to play it by ear in orienting your subordinates. The more lax the work environment, the more propensity there is to abuse office privileges. What is your company's policy on:

Coffee Breaks
Visiting
"Telephonitis"
Poor Business Manners
Collections and Contributions
Personal Hygiene and Neatness

Coffee Breaks

Find out whether the coffee break is to be used for a meal, socializing, orientation, or whatever. Is it limited to a short respite for beverages to be partaken at the work scene with slight work interruption?

Now compare the conduct of your subordinates with that of their fellow workers in other departments. Are they out of line? Consult with your superior or plan to discuss it at the next conference on management problems. You may be surprised to learn that other executives have trouble because of *your* laxity with your subordinates.

Visiting

Office visiting, if uncontrolled, can wreak havoc with the best planned work schedules, and reflect unfavorably on those in charge.

For more years than anyone cared to remember, Mrs. Hilary Craig had been file mistress in a certain firm. By now she was a company fixture, making it hard to cope with her disturbing fondness for visiting. As guest or hostess, she frequently deprived disgruntled managers and supervisors of their subordinates' assistance.

What Was Done

A frustated but inventive executive decided to try a little psychology on the intrepid old lady. He artfully implied to Mrs. Craig that she was falling behind with her records while letting "others" take up so much of her time. This appealed to Mrs. Craig's well-known pride in her work and wrought the desired effect where harsh measures may have failed or given birth to new problems.

Use a little imagination. Instead of greeting gabby co-workers with "How are you?", smile and wave a silent greeting. This ruse may also save your subordinates from unwanted visits.

To discourage visitors:

Stay Busy.

Keep your subordinates busy. If necessary, lend them out *reciprocally* to other shorthanded executives.

Telephonitis

Advanced telephonitis among subordinates can make strong executives quail, and is a continuing source of friction between management and personnel. On the executive level, it precipitated a minor crisis in one large trade association:

To accommodate the association's members and visitors, the management installed a public telephone booth.

Foster, an executive whose desk was next to the public telephone, soon realized the advantages to himself of this nearness to the pay booth. In no time he was receiving personal calls there, delaying outgoing messages and disturbing those convening in a nearby meeting room with the loud ringing of the bell.

At the next management conference, the following solutions were offered and discarded for the accompanying reasons:

1. Lay down a rule forbidding staff employees to receive incoming calls? Too difficult to enforce without setting off a chain of related disciplinary problems.
2. Take out the public phone? No, it was a good idea to provide this service for members and visitors.
3. Place the booth in the meeting room? Impractical because it would interfere with meetings, be awkward to reach, etc.

What Was Done

The pay booth was relocated close to the operator's switchboard in the entrance corridor, taking it away from Foster's location. A memorandum was also issued to the staff informing them that thereafter all incoming calls to the pay booth would be answered by the operator only.

There may not be a cure for telephonitis short of firing the chronic offender, but in these days of skilled labor shortage, it pays to try positive control methods.

Why Not a "Save Money Campaign"? Invite employees to offer practical suggestions. You may be astonished to learn how readily your subordinates accept restrictions of their own choosing!

A questionnaire entitled, "How to Diagnose Telephonitis," might be set up along these lines:

How many personal calls do I make a day? 3 _____
5 _____ more _____
How many were necessary? _____
If I make more than x number of calls, why? Bored
_____, unoccupied _____, worried _____, other _____.
How much money does it add up to? _____
Would I resent it if the management deducted the
amount from my pay? _____
Am I aware that I lose whenever my company loses
money? _____

You can play around with this theme and come up with ideas of your own that fit your work group and environment.

There is such a thing as being *too subtle*, as a good friend of mine found out:

Ed's telephone is literally the lifeline of his small but profitable recording business. His excellent secretary and Jill-of-all-trades was once seriously afflicted with telephonitis, causing Ed to lose his hair along with his clients. Too soft (or "chicken") to reprimand her, he resorted to all manner of devious ruses, even leaving the telephone bills prominently displayed for her benefit.

Finally he prevailed upon a client at RCA to write him a very strongly worded letter protesting that his inability to reach Ed on the phone had forced him to seek out a competitor. Triumphantly waving this missile at his secretary, Ed at last put across his message.

Look at the time-consuming subterfuge for what could have been quickly accomplished by simply telling her what was expected.

Poor Business Manners

Poor business manners are often caused by nothing more than ignorance. Your subordinates must know what you want. They also mirror your behavior; a desirable image of them is a flattering picture of yourself. How do your subordinates make you look?

A sloppy image of you is a poor advertisement for your firm, as one young executive ruefully learned. Away from his desk one day, he was shocked to hear his subordinate call loudly across the room to him, "Hey boss, some joker here wants to talk to you on the phone." The "joker" heard, and before our friend could reach his desk, the offended client had decided to take his business elsewhere.

A hand over the mouthpiece of a telephone is an unreliable shield. Sound can travel from the receiver to the transmitter. To effectively block sound from a caller, both transmitter and receiver must be covered.

Telephone manners are especially important. "Good morning, Mr. Smith's office" is preferable to the non-committal "Hello," because it is more pleasing and establishes instant identification. If your telephone is equipped to handle more than one call, show your secretary at the outset how to properly manipulate the instrument. Callers should never be left dangling or be made to feel they are getting the "brush-off."

Your own manners make a difference!

Mrs. DeGerard who is in charge of the dining room of the Wychmere Harbor Club in Massachusetts charmingly sets the mood and pace for her young helpers. Each morning when they report for work, the college students are greeted with a cheery "Good morning, are you ready to go to work for us?" Their "Yes ma'am," is followed up by a courteous, "Please have your breakfast. It is served." In turn the guests are treated in the same gracious manner. *Result:* A gratifying and profitable full house all the time.

Collections and Contributions

Employee collections and contributions can become a source of embarrassment or aggravation to employees. Perhaps you can't shield them from solicitations for engagements, weddings, new babies, anniversaries or retirements, but at least keep outside agencies away from the work area.

What about those "do-gooders" from whom you are seldom spared? Try this:

Permit *only* authorized collections.

Post a record of number and type of collections.

Set up a general fund or "kitty" with withdrawals subject to general agreement.

NOTE: All donations are strictly voluntary.

Personal Hygiene and Neatness

Personal hygiene and neatness problems must be handled delicately. It is a rare executive who does not shy away from this disciplinary area. But unclean clothing, body odors, feet on desks, messy work areas, and littered rest rooms are intolerable social offenses.

What to do:

1. Initiate a regular program of communications presenting various aspects of personal hygiene and housekeeping.
2. Prominently display cartoons or other humorous "hints."
3. Convey the desired personal image as an integral part of management.

Don't wait until your subordinates take matters into their own hands.

In one company a personal hygiene problem retrogressed to such a point that the girls began leaving anonymous notes on the desk of the offending worker. His constant clearing of his throat with the accompanying unpleasant connotations had become intolerable to his co-workers. Although the man took note and subsequently controlled his affliction through medical aid, the workers' intervention had shown up the leader's ineptitude.

Non-Aggression Pacts

In attempting to obtain greater output from a subordinate, Bill Keating felt justified in harshly reprimanding him. Greatly offended, the worker went over Bill's head, of course extolling his own merits and company loyalty. He charged that Bill never looked ahead and impatiently assigned new tasks before current ones were completed. Without digging any further into the matter, the manager excused the smug complainant and counseled Keating to improve his supervisory know-how. The result was a "stand-off" or non-aggression pact between Bill and his subordinate, with each one thereafter giving the other a wide berth.

A very common non-aggression pact is one between an executive and his secretary who shield each other. Such an alliance almost cost young Grady Rankin his job:

One day when Grady was at the World Series instead of attending a sales meeting, his secretary, Helen "covered" for him by saying that Grady was out sick. Gratefully, Grady began to allow Helen the same privileges enjoyed by older secretaries of leaving early and reporting late. He failed, however, to reckon with the "companyitis" of two old-timers who resented Helen's "seizure" of their "exclusive" privileges.

Early one afternoon when Grady was absent but his boss was not, the two cronies made a great show of closing shop for the day. Unwittingly, Helen followed suit, giving the plotters their chance to reappear and report her to the department manager.

When called on the carpet about Helen's behavior, Grady gallantly jumped to her defense. The more he defended her, the worse he looked, and it was many months before he repaired his image in the eyes of his superiors.

It is easy enough to control your own participation in non-aggression pacts by adhering to a strict policy of non-involvement. But coping with alliances among your subordinates is something else again. As in so many discipline areas, prevention has the positive effect of reducing or eliminating the need for corrective actions.

It helps to know *why* workers enter into voluntary non-aggression pacts with one another. Mainly, such allegiances are:

1. Primarily defensive
2. Protests against regimentation

3. The need to "get away" with something
4. A way to "belong"

What to do:

1. Reduce the need for defensiveness by establishing a congenial work climate where each worker knows he will get a "square deal." Make your presence spell "refuge" as well as "authority" to your subordinates.
2. Camouflage regimentation by giving your helpers some voice in their direction. Occasionally solicit and follow their suggestions.
3. Delegate responsibility to capable subordinates.
4. Praise, praise wherever merited.
5. Play fair and your subordinates won't feel they must "get away" with something. Be impartial and consistent in enforcing rules and imposing penalties. Don't pull "sneak" tactics in announcing work schedules, assigning overtime, making transfers, arranging vacations, etc.

A worker's need for group identity furnishes you with raw material of the utmost potential for channelling your subordinates' behavior. Learn to work through group representation to promote company goals and to develop your own executive potential. Become a trustworthy link between your workers and management, and you make yourself a key figure in the organization.

In the absence of organized worker groups, give your subordinates group identity by helping them to form clubs or societies based upon compatible social, ethnic or religious interests.

INSUBORDINATION

Don't be surprised to uncover a bit of the latent insubordinate in all employees! You must, however, distinguish between a flagrant refusal to comply with a rightful command and a worker's temporary inability to carry out orders because of hurt pride, illness, weariness or emotional disturbance.

There is nothing subtle about insubordination—it is a serious offense that must be corrected for the sake of group morale and of achieving organization objectives. As an instrument for weeding out incompetents and insubordinates, discharge can be viewed as a *positive* means of forestalling future disciplinary problems—as a last resort.

How to Deal with Insubordination

1. Correctly diagnose the action as insubordination.
2. Be sure you have all the facts!
3. Seek your superior's guidance.
4. Try counseling.

Your boss should back you up even when you err in dealing with a subordinate, but don't count on it! Rely on the *facts* to justify your charges of insubordination. Simply saying, "He is insubordinate," or "He is a troublemaker," will not (and should not) carry much weight before a dismissal committee. Remember that every time you must fire someone, you are putting your own competency on the line.

Preston R. Murray was in charge of a division for a company manufacturing precision tools. Of all his group, McCabe was the only maverick, walking off the job whenever he chose. When summoned back to his duties, McCabe would insolently wait until he had finished his smoke or chat, visibly dragging his feet. Reprimands had no effect. The day of reckoning came when Preston chanced upon McCabe apparently just sitting around wasting time in the cafeteria. This was the last straw, and Preston fired him immediately.

At the dismissal hearing, McCabe righteously pleaded that he had received no assignment on that day. It was the truth, but Preston had been too inflamed at the time to check up on this. Also, he had failed to keep a record of McCabe's many infractions or to consult with his own superior. The hearing became a contest of Preston's word against McCabe's. In the absence of tangible evidence against him, McCabe was reinstated, and both men were counseled to "bury the hatchet."

Is It Your Attitude?

Personnel conflicts often arise out of nothing more than someone "rubbing you the wrong way" and vice versa.

A few years ago in the national headquarters building of a prominent publishing firm, the president wanted to fire an elevator operator in the building because he didn't like the worker's attitude. The latter was not inclined to be sociable and would stare churlishly ahead never acknowledging the presence of his passengers, distinguished or not.

At the hearing, the operator's union decided that unsociability was not ground for dismissal, since the worker had been hired as an elevator operator and not as an official greeter.

How to Prevent Insubordination

1. Let your subordinates know that you can and will report insubordination.
2. Instruct workers thoroughly in their duties.
3. Substitute a conversational manner for the direct issuance of orders.
4. Appear to be "helping" rather than directing or countermanding.
5. Give competent employees some voice in their work.
6. Overlook minor infractions, but generously praise achievement.
7. Develop qualified candidates for key positions so that you have no "indispensable" worker.
8. Enforce (consistently and fairly) the rules and policies.

When you give employees a voice in their work, you have to be very careful lest you *create* insubordination instead of controlling it. Suppose that you have decided to act upon a subordinate's helpful suggestion and you talk it over with him beforehand. In executing the idea, your subordinate innovates an unauthorized "improvement" or two. This could be disastrous, since few subordinates are trained to evaluate the overall operations and to visualize the net results. Or the heady experience of having been once consulted can lead your subordinate to expect you to call him in on every little decision affecting him. Now he thinks he does not have to follow instructions unless you "clear it" with him first. He may begin to feel "better" than his co-workers, perhaps even singled out for a promotion which may be outside your jurisdiction to grant. Before you know it—insubordination!

Right from the start establish a policy of consulting with your helpers only when there is something worthwhile to be gained—in other words when you need their assistance and cooperation in formulating new work schedules, expediting production, reducing errors, etc.

Transfers and Promotions Are Positive Control Tools

There is no getting away from it—money is a great incentive for desirable performance. The prospect of increased earnings looms large in the minds of most workers. To some, status and praise mean as much as or more than money, especially to those who are looking up.

Along with raises and promotions, transfers, discharges and demotions are powerful control tools which can have negative as well as positive effects. It is easy to see the plus side of a promotion—you are almost certain to please the one advanced. Less apparent are the negative effects of an employee's promotion upon his co-workers who are "left behind." The advancement of "incompetents" can spawn related disciplinary problems.

Where you are responsible for the changed status of your subordinates, see to it that:

> Employees understand thoroughly the company's procedure for promotions, transfers, dismissals or demotions.
> Wherever possible, promotions go to workers who, because of past performance, have *earned* the promotion. (At lower levels, seniority may be a controlling factor.)

Not All Workers Want Promotions. Some are thoroughly satisfied to do a good job at their own comfortable level and do not desire additional responsibility.

Bill Chapman had a young foreman, Tony Morrelli, who ably supervised a crew of thirty men. When the plant grew to where additional management personnel was needed, Bill had no trouble "selling" Tony as a candidate, but when he went to Tony with the good news, Bill was floored by his refusal to accept the promotion. Tony wanted no new responsibilities that would overlap into his leisure hours.

What to do in a case like this:

Reward good workers who do not want promotions with bonuses, raises, praise and other forms of recognition.

Provide fringe benefits in the form of status symbols—a seat by the window, a private locker, a water flask, or whatever means the worker is "in."

Cherish faithful performers who, though not world-beaters, are nonetheless the backbone of many organizations.

Why Transfers?

A company's growth or decline, its change of geographical location, innovations, a worker's ailments, family troubles, personality conflicts, age or desire for advancement are but a few of the many and worthy reasons that lead management and employees to seek transfers.

Watch out for grievances and employee turnover triggered by unwise transfers. Are you cloaking a serious disciplinary problem in that transfer? Passing the buck will not help if your real problem is that you are incapable of probing in depth a conflict of interests.

Maybe it is your subordinate who wants the transfer. If so, then now is a good time to examine your own performance. Could be your lack of executive know-how is showing. Beware of a too obvious pattern of transferring misfits. That technique can hold you back, and is almost guaranteed to make you unpopular.

When a Transfer Is a Demotion

Used as a punitive measure a transfer is frequently a demotion which may be temporary or permanent, depending upon the circumstances. Ideally, the demotion should have the positive results of correcting the offensive behavior, in which case the "reformed" employee would then be eligible for a promotion.

Since there is nothing subtle about a demotion, most workers will recognize it for what it is. Therefore, even when this tactic is a necessary management expedient, consider it from all angles. Despite some of its undesirable aspects, do not overlook the positive effects of demotion as a control tool. Indeed it is sometimes the only way to satisfactorily resolve some problems.

For example, try painless demotion for relocating esteemed senior or handicapped employees. The Cleveland headquarters of Republic Steel Corporation has effectively accommodated such workers as receptionists and guides who perform a necessary service while greatly enhancing the company image.

Review

Executive control cannot be divorced from discipline, but discipline, either harsh or mild, is only one procedure by which you can control subordinates. If you try to motivate subordinates with threats, reprisals, etc., you will arouse their defensiveness and make them "fight" back.

Positive discipline (such as rewards), when intelligently used, can achieve desirable results without the unfavorable consequences of resentment, drop in rate of efficiency, lowering of morale and lack of cooperation. Reward to restrain as well as to compensate.

The failure of workers to comply with well established rules and policies of the firm indicates a lack of discipline—the leader is not in control.

Don't be afraid of your subordinates. Receptiveness to the suggestions of others should not entail giving up your right to make the decisions. *Your judgment should prevail.*

Use negative measures only when absolutely necessary. Situations requiring the use of absolute authority are rare when you have established positive control procedures.

Dismissals should be relegated to the background to be used as a last resort.

Insubordination, although a serious disciplinary problem, can be corrected and often avoided by the strategy of incentives, coaching, transfers, etc. When you must charge a worker with insubordination, be sure you have facts to substantiate it and the backing of your superior.

Fairness does not mean that you must deal identically with all workers. Dispense or withhold rewards among your subordinates according to their degree of performance, satisfactory or otherwise.

Use group psychology to orient and control subordinates through their desire to belong.

Positive discipline results in *effective control* of subordinates.

CHAPTER EIGHT

Get More from Your Subordinates
Through Counseling

"I'd do anything for my boss."
Isn't that the way you want your subordinates to feel about you?
Considerable research has unearthed the fact that most employees
like and respect their bosses. Liking the boss is also among the top
reasons given by workers for being satisfied with their jobs. Not
surprisingly workers rate their companies by their feelings for their
immediate supervisors. A "good company" can be generally trans-
lated into a "good boss" and vice versa.

What makes a good boss? Here are the answers given by workers
in widely scattered occupations:

1. My boss tells me what he expects from me.
2. My boss treats me fair and square.
3. I can go to the boss with my problems, personal as well as
   those on the job.
4. I always know what is going on.
5. The boss levels with me on job performance, rating, compensation and future prospects.

All the answers can be summed up with "The boss cares about
me."

Management know-how consists mostly of *ability to handle
people.* Job and technical knowledge are important at every stage,
but how you direct the talents and potential of others is the true
test of your executive skill.

151

It is a fact of life that no matter how you act everyone won't love you, but counseling is the "personal touch" that removes the chill from your relationships with your subordinates. Use this valuable tool to bring about desirable changes in the attitudes of employees who have perplexing job worries, are performing unsatisfactorily, are delinquent or are maladjusted.

Put Yourself in Your Subordinates' Shoes

Make it easy for your workers to approach you for guidance. Know their temperaments, abilities and aspirations and be willing to talk to them about what concerns them. Don't let aloofness, harshness or a quick temper scare your subordinates from seeking your counsel.

I know the president of a company that has a paternalistic policy of granting interest-free personal loans to employees upon the approval of the applicant's immediate superior. Much to his surprise, the president looked up from his papers one day to find one of the workers before him.

"May I see you about a personal loan, sir?" asked the employee. His son had recently died and he wanted to borrow the money for a grave marker.

"Why didn't you go through your supervisor?" the president wanted to know.

"I couldn't do that, sir," replied the worker. "I'd be on his list then like all the others. I came to you because I thought you would lend me the money without holding it against me."

Violating his own established policy, the president gave the worker the needed amount out of his own pocket, telling him to repay it whenever he could—which was gratifyingly soon.

Thus alerted to the supervisor's strong-arm tactics, the president instigated a quiet investigation that unearthed a distressingly low morale in that supervisor's department. The bullying executive was counseled to soft pedal his approach, or else.

Communication is a two-way street. Your subordinates are entitled to voice legitimate complaints. Listen, and if they are wrong show them politely where they err, demonstrating, if necessary.

BE A TRANQUILIZER

Sometimes a worker falls behind for no apparent reason:

Anton Ryder was a very capable accountant, but suddenly his records showed glaring inaccuracies. This continued for several days until Anton's boss had a talk with him and learned that the man's wife had recently undergone a serious operation. The added financial burden of medical expenses made it impossible for Anton to hire a nurse to assist his wife during her first days out of the hospital, and he was very worried about his wife alone at home in her weakened condition.

Anton's boss rose sympathetically to the occasion by arranging for Anton to take off the necessary time to stay with his wife at no reduction in pay. Ryder had been afraid to ask for the time off for fear of losing his wages. If his boss had not taken the initiative to approach Anton, the unfortunate situation might have continued until Ryder had to be discharged.

You will find counseling a valuable control tool to:

> Relieve workers' anxieties.
> Inform.
> Teach.
> Motivate.
> Discipline positively.
> Evaluate work performance.

Most of us experience anxieties directly associated with our work—both real and imaginary. The amount and type of anxiety are often determined by our needs, regardless of our status in the organization. At the lower levels, for example, there will be more apprehension occasioned by the basic human wants of food and shelter as related to continuous employment and security.

Numerous other unseen factors not directly associated with job functions are also constantly in force and inevitably influence each individual. Be on the lookout for these manifestations of anxiety that can affect the performance of your subordinates:

> Hostility (outright or subtle).
> Failure to yield the desired output.
> Day-dreaming.
> Nervousness (sometimes resulting in accidents to self or others).
> Quality of work (unusually good or poor).
> Repeated absences or lateness.
> Over-zealousness in arriving early or staying late.

E. J. Foley was number one man in his group, and he knew it. Whenever Foley was absent from the scene there was a visible lag in production. The inevitable occurred—Foley became cocky and overbearing. He was the indispensable man and began to take advantage of his fortuitous situation to primarily satisfy his ego.

Then one day a promising newcomer joined the group, and the supervisor began to groom him as a "key man." Anything but slow witted, Foley immediately rose to the challenge, demonstrating so effectively his leadership ability that he became supervisor when his boss moved up the executive ladder.

Some job anxiety is good for effective work performance, but the degree of anxiety needed for maximum yield varies from individual to individual and from job to job. The stress of unexpected competition drives some to alcoholism, chain smoking, or other harmful excesses. Anxiety is obviously too high when either health or performance is adversely affected. Overanxiety is sometimes manifested by physical disorders such as ulcers, nervousness, headaches, etc.

Recognize that aside from their purely personal problems, your workers are concerned about:

> Communications (keep them informed).
> Continuity of employment.
> Compensation (both absolute and relative).
> Training.
> Fair play.
> Status.
> Belonging.

The negative aspects of job anxieties are increasingly prevalent with workers experiencing more and more difficulty in yielding the desired performance. Learn to recognize the urgent, psychological needs of your subordinates so that you can help them to achieve your company's objectives.

Use counseling to help your workers to adjust to their jobs and environment. Let them know you care. Through prudent counseling you can often prevent blow-ups and divert pent-up emotions toward the desired objectives.

DON'T LET YOUR SUBORDINATES OPERATE IN A VACUUM

Make it a habit to be the first in getting to your subordinates with news and pertinent information about them and their jobs.

Stop rumors before they grow. Your workers are always concerned about impending changes—whether it be change of location, renovations, where they will sit, etc.

I once worked in a building where the elevator operators were being replaced by self-service cars over a prolonged period. The management had not bothered to inform the operators when they would be replaced, about termination allowances, or future prospects of steady employment. The operators' mounting apprehension as the work progressed was painfully visible to all who came and went in the building.

Their worry brought on illness (real and imaginary) that soared the rate of absence, and service became so poor that many of the building's tenants refused to renew their leases, and new tenants were not attracted. Failing to connect their losses with their pitiless personnel policy, the owners of that building paid a fancy price for their oversight.

The individual worker is seldom the only one affected when he is unemployed. Counsel your subordinates on any impending cut of staff or expenses, so that if they must, they can be on the lookout for other employment. Especially, let your workers know from the beginning if a job is only temporary.

Make Your Workers Feel That They "Belong"

Unless your subordinates feel that they "belong" they cannot produce to their full capacity. A worker's concern for achieving the objective must parallel that of the other members of the work team.

In one large shipping company, the women packers have the custom of gathering at two tables at one end of the cafeteria for lunch and coffee breaks. Newcomers are usually welcomed to the "inner circle" within the first week. Wanda Hale, however, was still eating alone a month after she started to work.

Her solitary figure attracted the attention of Mrs. Lewis, her supervisor. Why, she pondered, was Wanda being shunned by her co-workers? A shrewd observer, Mrs. Lewis soon noted that, while the other women wore loose-fitting, practical work smocks, Wanda dressed in tight-fitting sweaters and short skirts. These did not go unnoticed by the male employees, to the obvious chagrin of the other women.

Mrs. Lewis joined the lonely girl at her table, where encouraged by her superior's interest, Wanda confided that she was seriously contemplating looking for another job. After a few friendly talks, Mrs. Lewis tactfully prevailed upon Wanda to dress more like the rest of her group and also counseled the girl on company customs and policies. Wanda cooperated, and although she never could completely camouflage her comely attributes, she was soon "one of the girls." There was also this interesting side effect: The other women began to wear make-up and more attractive work clothes.

Status Is Very Important to Most People. A simple matter of where one sits or hangs his coat can mean more to some workers than how much money he earns.

Inform present workers about an addition or replacement before the newcomer arrives, and speed up his acceptance by not having him appear in the group as a total stranger. If you foresee that a new employee will not be accepted by the group because of his ethnic or other background, make necessary transfers or hire an additional worker so there will be at least one person on the work scene that can identify with him.

COMPENSATION IS MORE THAN SPECIFIC WAGES PAID FOR SPECIFIC DUTIES

Your subordinates are concerned about fringe benefits as well as salary. Know the benefits offered by your organization, as well as those of competitors and other firms of like size and kind.

In addition to financial remuneration, workers also expect compensation in the form of praise, status, fair treatment, congenial work environment and a sympathetic and understanding management. Can you knowingly counsel your subordinates on vacations, holidays, sick leaves, pensions, and coffee breaks in terms of cost to management and value to employees?

Give Credit Where It Belongs. Some executives find it quite difficult to give praise to worthy employees. If your subordinate's idea is good enough to use—you look good too!

George, an electrical engineer now outstanding in his field, left one company because of lack of recognition for his contributions to its success. At the time, his immediate superior took full credit for all of George's valuable suggestions. The last straw was when he went directly to the firm's president with a suggestion for a major innovation, only to find it later presented as an idea of the president.

Consequently, George went to a major competitor of that firm, which has duly recognized his profitable contributions. The result was good for George—bad for his small-minded former employer.

Look Ahead for Your Subordinates. Coach and inspire them in their efforts at self-improvement. For example, you could encourage a typist to take instructions in shorthand, bookkeeping, or business machine operation. Some of your workers may need only a gentle push to finish high school, college or other education. When counseling on self-development, have available a list of schools or institutions, courses, time given, location, etc., where the necessary skills may be learned. A highly trained, competent work team shows off your management know-how.

Fresh out of high school, Ted Schumacher went to work in the mailing room of a large toy manufacturing company. He had been an honor student throughout school, and had won several scholarships. Unfortunately, Ted could not take advantage of these opportunities because of family obligations. Ted had to start earning money right away.

Recognizing Ted's potential, management lost no time in enrolling him in their executive training program. Ted was financially encouraged to take some college courses in the evening, and at 21 he showed noteworthy progress.

About the same time, however, he began to evince nervousness and inattention to the details of his job. More than once his superior would catch him gazing absently out the window. If suddenly approached, Ted would start visibly, then fumble ineffectually with the papers on his desk.

Knowing that management was concerned about this young man's continued growth, his superior undertook to counsel him. In the course of their informal talks, his superior learned that because of Ted's deep responsibility to his family's needs, he missed out on most of the fun of the other young people his age. Ted was a veritable recluse. Recently, however, he had received an invitation to a "blind date."

Ted wanted very much to accept, but he was terrified at the prospect. He couldn't dance, didn't know where to go, and didn't even know what to say to girls. His boss told Ted that he used to feel terrible when it seemed everyone laughed at his first attempts to skate—until he started laughing along with them. Then he suggested that Ted take dance instructions at the local "Y" where there would also be other beginners.

Now Ted Schumacher is a vice-president of his company, and his former boss heads up the organization's executive training program.

Direct vs. Non-Direct Counseling

There are two types of counseling—direct and non-direct. In direct counseling *you* determine the areas in which the worker needs help. You do most of the talking, which has the disadvantage of putting the worker on the defensive. On the other hand it has the distinct advantage of dealing directly with the problem, as you see it.

For example, Joe Smith's excuses for his repeated absences are becoming less credible with each new one, you decide the time has come to have it out with Joe. There is nothing to be gained here by beating around the bush. You point out the problem to Joe and agree to let bygones be bygones, because you are counting on him to shape up after this.

Use direct counseling for "on the spot" correction of simple infractions and for safety purposes.

Unlike direct counseling in which you emphasize present conditions, the non-direct method is directed toward your subordinate's growth in self-understanding, which can help him to overcome future problems on the job. Thus, instead of plastering over the present problem and dealing with symptoms, non-direct counseling enables you to tackle the core of the anxiety.

Take Frank Jones who is obviously drinking too much, and carrying his hangovers onto the job scene. This problem will not yield to a one-time treatment. This calls for a series of non-direct counseling to help you both reach a better understanding of the underlying causes.

Barney Ellis will always be grateful to the supervisor who helped him to fight alcoholism by sending him to the plant physician, then counseled him throughout Barney's trying period of fighting his weakness. While undergoing treatment, Barney was transferred temporarily to a less taxing job. His boss continued to encourage him when Barney was ready to give up the whole thing. Now Barney is back in the mainstream.

Be prepared to counsel your subordinates on a wide variety of subjects. Don't be surprised to hear:

Where is the best place for me to live?

How should I budget my income?

Who is a good doctor, dentist, insurance man, etc.?

What's a good school for my children?

Do the best you can to offer assistance in these matters, but keep in mind that your counseling role is mainly to orient your subordinates so that their outlook will be compatible with your company's policies, the work environment, training and other aspects of their jobs. Many things cannot be changed, but attitudes can be altered —yours and theirs.

In a leading book publishing firm, a young, new Art Director was so approachable that she found herself besieged for guidance on every little work detail, including personal problems—so much so, that she had to work overtime to perform the work for which she had been hired.

There is such a thing as being too sympathetic and helpful to your subordinates. It is better for you, them and your company if they can work alone.

Unless you have been hired specifically as a counselor, consultations with your subordinates should not become a full-time job. You should, however, know the techniques of non-direct counseling so you will be better able to explore and alleviate the less apparent causes of undesirable behavior. Indirect counseling urges the worker to reach "his own" solution and at most demands only a reasonable amount of skill and tact. Basically, the clue to successful non-direct counseling is to listen carefully as the worker talks about his problem as he sees it, pinpoints the real difficulty and thinks of ways to correct the situation.

How to Counsel

Don't attempt to counsel until you take this pledge:

1. I do not have ultimate control of any subordinate.
2. I am not qualified to decide the *one* best action for a subordinate, except where directly associated with job performance.

3. I will not practice amateur psychiatry.
4. I will counsel in private wherever feasible.
5. I will respect all confidences of a purely personal nature.

Success in counseling hinges on your ability to speak man to man in private to your subordinate in a friendly, informal manner. The creation of the proper atmosphere is immeasurably helpful. Be ready to listen to what is on your subordinate's mind, but retain and exercise your prerogative to specify the desired action where your subordinate is unable to discern the problem.

When undertaking non-direct counseling, try this success formula:

> Prepare in advance.
> Listen more than you talk.
> Look for the meaning behind the words used.
> Establish rapport.
> Avoid personal involvement.
> Help the worker to achieve insight.

Prepare in Advance

Before scheduling an appointment with a subordinate, collect all available information on every aspect of the worker's background, including vital statistics and past work performance. Review and discuss his work load and attitude with others for whom he may have worked. An up-to-date chart on each worker can be very useful to you in determining his motivating factors—an essential requisite of effective counseling. In trying to appraise the worth of a subordinate you have to make a factual analysis of both his contribution and the job performed.

A very skilled worker can make a difficult job seem easy, while a less capable employee may have trouble executing the simplest duties. You have to consider:

> Job knowledge.
> Performance.
> Judgment (sound reasoning in the absence of detailed instructions).
> Ability to get along with others (above, at the same level, and below).

Amount of help he needs for adequate performance.
Degree of responsibility.

Your subordinates rightfully expect that their job performance will be evaluated for possible promotion to a higher level. Be ready to counsel your assistant about his job performance in terms of:

His strengths and weaknesses.
His future prospects.
What changes he needs to make so as to increase his worth to the company.
What actions management will take to help him achieve his full work potential.

I recall being fired from a manual type of job when management learned that part of my pay was set aside for a college education. On the other hand, for over twenty years a generous employer spared no reasonable expense in assisting me and other workers in our self-development programs.

Unless you have all the facts, your judgment may be based upon emotions and impulses—unreliable yardsticks. When a worker is not performing desirably, take time out to *find out why*. In particular, investigate those factors that make up his work environment. Does he have adequate equipment, etc.? Outside factors may be at fault, because unavoidably a worker carries his personal problems into the work area, and likewise takes home the experiences and heartaches of the job environment.

Listen More Than You Talk

You counsel to improve performance by shedding light on your subordinate's behavior. This is not always easy to do, because the worker may have inhibitions coupled with an inability to communicate clearly. The best help that you can give him is to listen attentively. Forget your own serious problems for now and concentrate your attention upon your subordinate; he can tell when your mind is not on his difficulties.

If a subordinate bogs down while groping for the right words or even comes to a dead stop, do not fill these gaps. Quite the contrary, an inane remark of yours may cause a break in the worker's train of thought, thereby reducing the value of the counseling session. Above all, refrain from criticizing or complaining while your subordinate is trying to gather his thoughts.

Look for the Meaning Behind the Words

Do not always take a subordinate's words at face value; learn to discern what he means rather than what he says.

Be careful not to steer the worker or put words into his mouth. Openly anticipating his thoughts can put him on the defensive.

Help him focus his attention on those factors preventing satisfactory performance.

Establish Rapport

A pleasant manner helps to put your subordinate at ease. Don't be pompous, condescending or paternalistic.

If you think criticism is necessary, don't present it as such, and be sure to praise first.

Don't compare one worker's performance to that of another; this can build up resentment to both you and the lauded employee.

Your subordinates need to feel that you know and can understand their actions, emotions, desires and fears. You cannot afford the protective shield of aloofness or coldness.

Mr. W. F. Cranston, president of a large service company, was so sensitive to the needs of others that he isolated himself from his employees and literally shut the door of his office to their problems. The intermediate executives had to cope with their subordinates without involving the president.

Yet, when unavoidably drawn in, Mr. Cranston had been known to show deep understanding and generosity. As soon as the crisis passed, however, he lost no time retreating back into his protective shell. Before grateful employees could so much as say "thank you," he had already slammed shut his door—as if he regretted having extended a helping hand.

Since Mr. Cranston was head of his organization, he felt free to extend or withdraw himself as he saw fit, but this trait kept even his highest paid subordinates from approaching him or exploring with him their long-range goals or problems. Often, he was the last to know when one of his executives had decided to leave the firm.

This powerful organization began to fall apart at the seams, and its board of directors took another look at Mr. Cranston. In the interest of the company's continued growth, it was decided that the president would have to "open his door," or yield to someone who would.

Avoid Personal Involvement

Remain impartial by avoiding emotional involvement in a subordinate's personal problems. Otherwise, your partiality will show up as favoritism or prejudice. This is probably the greatest pitfall for the unwary, inexperienced young supervisor as he engages in counseling.

Henry C. Bates discovered this when it was almost too late. Henry was intelligent, capable and responsible, but woefully inexperienced when he found it necessary to counsel his pretty young stenographer.

Miss Bennett had many personal problems that were impeding her work performance. Although competent enough, she was very insecure and apprehensive. Henry perceived her need for counseling and endeavored to help.

But, unable to remain impartial, Henry became deeply enmeshed in the young woman's private life before he found out that she was seriously disturbed and had been undergoing professional treatment prior to her present employment. The end was that Bates was unable to be of any real help to Miss Bennett, who soon left the company in search of another sympathetic ear, but not before Henry had come perilously close to losing his coveted position—and his wife.

Achieve Insight

The process of non-direct counseling is directed toward your subordinate's gaining insight—the true recognition of one's self and the acceptance of that self. Ideally, with acceptance of self there comes a desire to control those factors which retard or prevent the desired behavior.

You and your subordinate will have reached a true understanding of what makes him "tick" if, through your counseling, you have helped him to recognize the root of his problem. Your success can, therefore, be measured in terms of his ability to:

1. Disregard what others think or say that he can achieve.
2. Recognize his own shortcomings.
3. Evaluate what he has actually accomplished by his own efforts.

4. Desire self-improvement.

5. Follow a course of action that will achieve the desired goals.

Of course you are not always going to have the time to sit around while your subordinates reveal their inner selves. You have your own specific work contributions to make.

The solution is to evolve a personal technique that encompasses a combination direct/non-direct counseling, striving not to become the recipient of unsolicited and unwanted confidences. Don't turn a deaf ear to your subordinates' personal problems, but limit your counseling to improving worker performance on the job.

GRIPES ARE OFTEN SMOKE SCREENS

Undesirable behavior often is indicative of deep personality problems that cannot always be corrected by a pat on the back or other ego-boosting techniques. See how effective non-direct counseling was in this case:

After eight years, Elliott Markham was still contentedly manning the same operation. When new employees were hired, Elliott was the one selected to show them around, and this pleased him very much. Although not officially designated, he was really second in command, because he enjoyed the special confidence of his superior. Since Markham was a general favorite among the other workers, they did not resent this added prestige that gave Elliott such visible pleasure.

Through the years, there had been no opportunity for advancing Elliott, who, although very capable, had never graduated from high school. Nevertheless, his supervisor was always on the lookout to "do something" for his well-liked assistant. By dint of persistent effort he finally manipulated Elliott into an opening in another department at an attractive increase in salary.

The new work area was larger and cleaner. There were better prospects for the workers there than in Elliott's previous location. Yet, it was not long before Elliott began to grumble and complain. At first it was too drafty in his new quarters, then it was unbearably close. He complained that he was expected to be back on the job before he had eaten his lunch, and that there was altogether too much pressure upon him to yield unreasonably high output. The constant griping was having its toll on the other workers who also began to feel "put upon" by management.

Thoroughly exasperated, Elliott's new boss was tempted to fire him, but hesitated in deference to the worker's long satisfactory service. He, therefore, sought out Elliott's former supervisor, who promised to talk with Elliott.

That talk stretched out into several counseling sessions before the real source of Elliott's problem came to light.

"I just don't feel right among that go-getter bunch," Elliott confessed one time.

"That boss just stands around staring at a fellow until he makes shivers run up my spine."

"It sure is nice having that extra pay, though," he further confided. "My wife had been putting off having her teeth fixed for a long time, and now she can go to the dentist, regular."

"I sure miss working for you. I used to be somebody then."

Gradually, Elliott came to realize that his griping stemmed from an insecurity that made him feel uncomfortable around the more aggressive and competitive workers in the new department. He also missed the friendliness of his former co-workers and the status of being the boss's right hand man.

In the course of the counseling, Elliott himself came up with the idea that if he concentrated more on doing a good job, the boss standing around would not bother him nearly as much. Elliott also gained a new appreciation for his increased earnings and the beneficial changes they brought to his family.

Elliott's former superior then went to the new boss and briefed him on the worker's emotional conflict. Once Elliott's boss started to show Elliott some sincere appreciation, his subordinate started to thaw. Eventually Elliott became acclimated to his new surroundings, and the added recognition coupled with his fatter pay envelope helped to compensate for his lost "status."

As a rule the chronic griper is an insecure individual seeking reassurance. If not allowed to reach extremes, the airing of grievances can be a healthy outlet for pent-up emotions, as well as an accurate barometer of serious trouble in the making.

Give prompt and friendly attention to expressed dissatisfactions, because repressed grievances among employees are frequently more damaging to general morale than those that reach the ears of management.

Plan ahead for those inevitable gripes by providing suggestion boxes and arranging for conferences with your superior when you feel subordinates are determined to go over your head. Complaints about poor lighting, inadequate washroom facilities, long hours, or burdensome schedules may be justified. At the very least they warrant investigation. Keep your eyes and ears open.

COUNSEL THROUGH GROUP REPRESENTATION

The smart executive soon learns how to deal constructively with worker representatives so as to promote the interests of both management and employees. Where your subordinates are organized in a union, you will find it a distinct advantage to have the goodwill of their representatives and to cooperate with them.

A top executive confided to me: "Am I glad to have supervisors to deal with union representatives in the shop. With my short temper, if I were out there directing the workers, I'd get in a fist fight every day. Those foremen can say, 'You so and so get back on the job,' and the men love him for it."

Work groups exert a strong influence on the individual members, and can often bring salutary pressure to bear upon the lax or insubordinate worker under your control. Employees identify strongly to group affiliations and often, being "left out" or shunned by other members is the most effective control measure of all.

Pete Archer had been supervisor of a punch press operation for three years, and was proud of his ability to handle men. He wanted to get ahead and took advantage of most opportunities to improve his managing technique. Mostly it had paid off—Archer ran a well organized, productive work unit and he seemed to have won the respect and cooperation of his men—all but one.

For some time now, Archer had tried his utmost to "get through" to John Berger, a very careless operator. He had tried private reprimands, cussing, suggestions, and even praise on those occasions when John performed satisfactorily, but there was no noticeable improvement. The pattern of carelessness and indifference to the quality of his work continued. The main trouble was that John was a sullen, taciturn man with whom Archer, try as he might, could establish no rapport.

Deciding upon a new approach, Archer waited for an opportunity to discuss his problem with Anderson, the shop steward. Since Anderson was overly protective of his group, Archer tried this ruse: "Is something bugging John these days? He can't seem to concentrate on his job. Is there some way that we can help him?"

Shrewd enough to perceive Archer's real intent, Anderson promised to look into the matter, because it was in the union's interest to keep up production standards. Within a few days John's work habits showed marked improvement.

Individual members will often submerge their own interests to that of their work group. It is not at all uncommon for members to put themselves out in order to make their group "look good."

You "have it made" when your workers are convinced that their work objectives are compatible with those of management. Your cooperation with the union leaders can help you achieve this eminently desirable objective.

Seek their assistance in explaining company policy to workers, as well as when handling awkward personnel problems. This will be a more effective technique after you have earned sufficient confidence to be in on the problems of your subordinates.

Your task will be immeasurably easier when it is the policy of your company to promote such cooperation. For example, Mr. N. J. Greene, President of the National Electric Coil Division of McGraw-Edison Company, has pointed this up in terms of worker attitude following two strikes six years apart. During the first, the company made an attempt to continue operation with a skeleton force—bitterness toward the company was harbored for an extended period after the strike was settled. During the latter strike, the company shut down all operations, except for the office staff.

Mr. Greene has stated that the marked improvement in the attitude of the workers after the latter strike is so great that a complete shutdown is expected in the event of a future strike at his plant.

Review

Counseling is an invaluable tool in directing subordinates who have perplexing job worries, are not doing their best, etc. Through counseling you can often secure the desired production while maintaining good morale and keeping strife down to a minimum.

Workers like to be noticed. Don't be afraid to talk to your subordinates about their performance. If a man comes to you with an idea for doing his job better, at least listen to him.

Listen. Hearing out a worker helps to ease his burden and often leads to helping him find his own solution. When you are unable to assist your subordinate, know where to direct him for the necessary guidance.

Keep your workers informed about all that concerns them.

Counsel in private, when and where feasible.

Encourage your subordinates to come to you with their problems by being approachable. Let them feel that together you can work out difficulties.

Stress a worker's abilities along with his shortcomings.

Let your subordinates be the first in broaching purely personal matters. Be sympathetic, but do not give specific guidance when by training or experience you are not adequately qualified to do so. Above all else, do not meddle or pry into the personal lives of your workers.

Respect your subordinates' confidences by never revealing any information of a personal or intimate nature not directly relevant to the job or general welfare of the organization.

Show You Care!

CHAPTER NINE

How to Thrive in Any Organizational Climate

It was Christmas Eve in a big city; a typical office party was in full swing. The meal had ended—but not the drinking. With every round of drinks the thawing-out process increased to a fine crescendo of warm goodwill to all. Most of the barriers were down—bosses were not only friendly with their subordinates, many were acting like pals (or more).

Carried away by the spirit of it all, one junior executive interrupted his immediate superior in the middle of an anecdote. "That's not how it was at all," the stimulated young man exclaimed. Then in a confidential aside to his neighbor, he added, "You have to tell it like it is." Whereupon, heedless of his superior's red face which belied an ominous sobriety in the midst of all the alcoholic congeniality, the brash young man told the story "right."

Right? All wrong, of course. It takes more executive know-how than job knowledge and competence to get ahead in business!

What is "right" in one work environment can be all wrong in another. You can possess a full measure of all the necessary executive attributes and still be a misfit if you do not recognize and identify with your organizational climate.

Fred Lehn, Executive Secretary for the International Executive Association and former Treasurer of Underwood, is one of those individuals who has moved steadily forward from the day he started, with scarcely a faltering step. So competent, reliable and

169

trustworthy that you can "set your clock by him," you would expect Fred Lehn to thrive in an organizational climate. Not so, claims Fred, recalling the time he was asked by a young dynamic president to make a clean sweep of the existing staff of long-time and dedicated older employees.

This was an action so against the grain of Fred's nature, that rather than compromise with his conscience, Fred relinquished his lucrative post.

"That's all very well," you say, "for a man of independent means, or another job to go to, but I have bills to pay, a family to support, etc." When you can't afford the luxury of just walking away from an undesirable situation, what then?

You bide your time but you don't waste it. Make the most of whatever environment you happen to be in.

Management techniques can be cultivated in any work area, regardless of size, the number of subordinates, or scope of supervision.

Even Josephine, manager of a breakfast bar with one assistant, must plan, organize, train, delegate responsibility, budget, and please clients—all management techniques—though on an unpretentious scale.

At the lower levels you also have certain advantages: Mistakes are less humiliating since fewer people are involved.

Between the ages of 20 and 30 you can afford to gather work experience for the future—in one, two, perhaps three work environments. At this stage you can take off in several directions without acquiring the stigma of "job hopper." So in your positions use each experience as a stepping stone to the goal you have set for yourself. *Experience* is your fundamental need at this time.

Due either to necessity or to a reluctance to change, most workers gradually adapt to their organizational climates. They soon make a comfortable niche for themselves where they dutifully grind out the required output to earn their daily bread. But *you* are ambitious; merely to adapt is not enough for you. You are going to *thrive* in your organizational climate with this growth formula:

1. Identify your organizational climate.
2. Recognize the best climate for you.
3. Play it straight with executive know-how.

What Is Your Organizational Climate?

Every organizational climate is some combination of four basic types: Autocratic, Bureaucratic, Democratic, and Idiocratic. To correctly diagnose your climate, study each one carefully, then blend until the mixture resembles your own work area.

AUTOCRATIC CLIMATE

The chief characteristic of the autocratic climate is its *rigid administration* which requires strict loyalty and compliance with the wishes of the chief executive. The auctocratic leader demands a free hand in his own actions, but his subordinates hear, "Do as I say."

The autocrat comes in many shapes and sizes, sometimes only thinly disguised as the "big daddy":

Roger P. Field, whose grandfather had founded the Fields Company, was carrying on the family tradition of company president and community leader. Nobody in that town could recall a time when a Field had not dominated the scene. The first Field "to make it big" had been an old tyrant, but his grandson refined that role to project what he believed to be a more amiable image. Roger's favorite phrase was "We are all one family here—your problems are my problems."

How true; there was nothing about Roger P. Field's employees hidden from his watchful eyes. All the rules were extensions of Roger's personality and preferences.

Drinking was not one of Roger's weaknesses, so woe to the executive who was ever found indulging. "Nothing personal, you understand, Smith, but we have to set an example. This is a dry town." You bet it is; it's Field's town.

The autocrat is a compulsive driver. He is capable of and often makes outstanding contributions, because he has a strong desire to express himself and to gain the maximum recognition for his efforts and knowledge.

To the autocrat, success is power. He likes to identify with authority and loves the phrase, "the big boss wants it." Only the uncompromisingly authoritative superior can command the respect from the autocratic worker.

To grow in an autocratic climate you must possess those characteristics which make it easy for you to adjust to it, such as self-effacement and awe of authority. You can thrive in such a climate if your personality is compatible with:

1. Laying down the law.
2. Lording it over others.
3. Specific orders or decrees rather than subtle leadership.
4. Imposing your will on others.
5. Overriding or discounting the wishes of others.
6. Making puppets of subordinates.
7. Insistence upon having it all your own way.

Bureaucratic Climate

By no means are bureaucracies restricted to the field of government; they are often found in those establishments where rules are regarded as sacred. Such rules may supersede good judgment in the evaluation of varying factors. Typically, a bureaucratic operation is recognizable by inflexible, hardheaded and formal measures of routine procedure (red tape) of administration.

The bureaucrat constantly strives to expand his scope of operations along existing lines, with any tendency to take in new areas construed as an encroachment on the prerogatives of others instead of as progress. This loyalty to consistent conformance, with its resultant personal security, creates a reluctance to launch new ventures.

Emotional security is the chief motivation; loyalty is demanded from subordinates. These two unrelenting pressures can alter the personality of subordinates—in effect, the leader's "brand" is usually stamped on the personnel of the company.

Both the bureaucrat and the bureaucratic organization can be generally recognized by these trademarks:

1. Written procedures which are repeatedly emphasized.
2. New or better ways of doing things do not justify deviating from the "tried and true."
3. Insofar as possible, independent thinking and judgment are discouraged.
4. If you try to break through with new approaches, you are likely to hear, "you're not being paid to think."

A West Virginia miner told me that whenever he saw posted a long list of work rules at the mine entrance, he automatically labelled it "not a good place to work."

A bureaucratic climate, therefore, provides an ideal atmosphere for you if you crave security and have unlimited capacity for loyalty.

DEMOCRATIC CLIMATE

Most people think of democratic as synonymous with fair play, and like to think of themselves as democratic persons. Actually, very few people are truly democratic in either their thinking or in their deeds. In fact, a purely democratic business administration is often neither the most practical nor the most effective means of achieving the overall objectives, i.e., making a satisfactory return on investment.

A democratic climate is seldom found in its pure form. Such a firm would be characterized by a total absence of snobbery, equal opportunities for all to advance, complete tolerance, equal distribution of power, with the freedom to express one's views and to act on individual responsibility.

Theoretically, in the democratic climate, each employee has a voice in the planning of his work with only enough direction to bring all relevant factors into balance. In actuality, the closest approximation to a democratic climate, however, is one where there is general consultation with others prior to decisions or actions which affect them.

The democratic leader usually yields to subordinates some of his undisputed rights with the expectation that greater benefits will thereby flow to his company. He tries to achieve maximum results by placing emphasis upon the cooperation by all personnel.

There is a wide gap, however, between the executive who practices democracy as a business technique to manipulate or orient his workers, and the one who is democratic by nature. The person with the cultivated democratic approach is generally more successful than his counterpart who has no other resources to draw upon under pressure. In other words, the democratic leader, as distinct from one using democratic techniques, will lean more toward a desire for popularity than for respect based upon effective performance. The authority of the true democrat emanates from the traditional respect for the position and not to his own person. His emotional security is usually related to how closely his actions parallel the needs of the group, rather than his own business concepts.

The truly democratic leaders listen to the ideas of others, and then endeavor to act in conformance with the views expressed. Wherever feasible, decisions are referred to subordinates—relevant factors and possible alternatives are presented for discussion.

Most businesses flourish by virtue of creative ideas and their implementation through appropriate actions. A democratic business climate usually obtains the best from its people while facilitating individual self-development.

A trade association, for example, almost has to be democratic. In a non-profit organization, the "profit" is how much the organization saves its members—be it in information collected or disseminated, market development, industry standards, or other legal activities.

Perhaps more than in industry, the trade association executive must be a "democrat." A thick skin helps too! He has to be able to persuade others and even influence their thinking—ideally without them knowing it. The trade association field is not, for instance, a fertile soil for the "steam roller" type of executive who might fit better in the advertising field. The right association executive is a willing "weeping post" and confidante of his industry—otherwise, he cannot serve to his full capacity.

The democratic organizational climate is ideal for you if you have:

1. A respect for individual dignity.
2. Belief in freedom for your subordinates.
3. Faith in your subordinates' ability and willingness to perform.
4. The capacity to detract from the significance of your own role.
5. A desire to align yourself with the members of your work team.

IDIOCRATIC CLIMATE (Manipulative, Psychological)

In the idiocratic climate, the individual worker is in the spotlight of leaders who use basic psychology to manipulate employees.

When the leader's knowledge of psychology is limited, he is often a shrewd individual who is a master of double talk.

The idiocrat knows that the ambitious, the sensitive, and the dedicated employee will usually pay a higher price for success, praise and status than an apathetic worker. Consequently you will find that an idiocratic leader is surrounded with "go getters" who are easy to orient because they want to please, and will try to outdo each other.

An idiocrat's sense of power is almost in direct proportion to his basic knowledge of his workers. Consequently, he leaves no stone unturned in his effort to ferret out their intrinsic values, idiosyncracies, genetics, predispositions, bias, inclinations, subjectiveness, etc.

Wherever possible the idiocrat plays the faults of one employee against another by delineating in "confidence" the gross or "stupid" errors of others. The subordinate is invited to "confess" on his superior, and vice versa.

If you are a politician, shrewd and intelligent, able to understand and use the underlying emotions of people (superiors, subordinates, and contemporaries), you will probably thrive in an idiocratic climate.

What Is the Best Climate for You?

You will find advancement easier where the climate is conducive to your executive development. Although a democratic climate is generally considered to be the most favorable for individual growth, it is not necessarily the best climate for your progress. In distinguishing and evaluating the various organizational climates, it is essential that you be honest and realistic enough to recognize the most compatible climate for you in terms of your talents, personality, goals, values, preferences, etc.

How Do You Fit In?

If you belong to the old school of business etiquette and dress, you will be uncomfortable where the executives loosen their ties, work in their shirt sleeves, put their feet on their desks, etc.

On the other hand, Mr. Harold R. Laubscher, Manager of the Chamber of Commerce of Gadsden, Alabama, once had the unhappy experience of being "underdressed." He was to appear before the Selection Committee of the Chamber of Commerce for

Fort Meyers, Florida, on a very hot Saturday afternoon. His predecessor had stressed the informality of the Committee members, so Harold left his coat in the car, only to find all the members sitting in an air-conditioned room *in coats.*

Harold didn't get that job.

You thrive best where you can be yourself without either sticking out like a sore thumb or getting lost in the crowd. When I received a medical discharge from the Armed Services during World War II, the tendered position in the local post office seemed made for me. While I was undergoing orientation, the postmaster cleared his throat and spat upon the floor. I never went back, and never for a moment regretted my decision—although at the time it seemed that there was no other way to earn my keep. Consequently, the phrase, "If you expect to rate, don't expectorate," has special meaning to me.

Erling Hughes was a good draftsman for his firm of Architectural Engineers. He liked his job, but he couldn't tolerate his associates' "deplorable" habit of chain smoking on the job. At first Erling tried to "reform" his associates with the none too subtle techniques of opening windows and fanning the air with paper, then desperately with a small humidifier on his desk.

All these ruses were met with outright indifference, or some jesting, until Hughes went too far. The day his co-workers found anti-smoking literature among their mail, the management decided that the firm of Architectural Engineers could dispense happily with the services of Erling Hughes—misfit.

Censoring or preaching to others is almost guaranteed to stifle your growth in any organizational climate.

If you can't or won't share the ways of your associates, at least look the other way. Don't snipe at them from the side lines.

To see if you fit in you have to understand the overall organization of your company, because it is the managerial structure that determines employee interrelations.

"It is a tradition that any institution is the lengthened shadow of one man." (From W. J. Donald, *Trade Associations.*)

Too often it is assumed that the climate of an organization also depends on one man. While it cannot be denied that the "top banana" is chiefly responsible for the prevailing mood of an environment, the nature of a business also contributes to the individual atmosphere of each organization.

Since togetherness is the basic characteristic of any group endeavor, the interrelations of all the people are the chief climate makers. Along with conditions and events, they are constantly changing too, so don't be too quick to decide that a certain climate is not for you.

"The world of business is never a Utopia," declares Mr. S. B. Kluger, General Manager of Eagle Electric Manufacturing Company. "Every executive position has its own inherent responsibilties, and every executive has to perform some acts that are contrary to his personal inclinations."

You may be thriving and not know it:

After eight years with Murdock Construction Company, Charles Quigley was ready to throw in the sponge. How long, reasoned Quigley, was a good man supposed to wait for recognition? Through the years Charles had studied nights until he finally earned his engineering degree, and now it seemed to him that management was coldly looking the other way.

So, Charles searched outside until he found a "junior" executive opening with more pay and some additional fringe benefits, and he left the Murdock Construction Company.

Quigley was next in line for an early and much better executive position than the one he settled for, but he never knew it. The Murdock management interpreted Quigley's outside search for advancement as disloyalty to the company and did not try to stop him with the good news Quigley had longed to hear.

Give your employer a chance to level with you before you decide to migrate to a "healthier climate," counsels H. N. Muller, former Vice-President of Westinghouse Electric Corporation.

Nothing will help you to thrive in your present climate like knowing how well off you really are!

If you do not have a better job lined up, then certainly take stock of your progress and your ultimate goal. Consider fully the risks and problems involved in a change (a bit of pessimism helps here). Carefully evaluate your present compensation, including all fringe benefits, before you are sure that you will be earning more in the new position. Ask yourself:

1. If I do get another job, will I be able to perform satisfactorily in an unfamiliar climate? In other words, am I adaptable?
2. Is my prospective employer the only one who is taking a chance? Do my qualifications justify my ambitions?
3. How old am I? Am I young enough (under 30) to hang around a while longer to see what may develop? If 45 or older, what are my present company's fringe benefits (life insurance, hospitalization, retirement, etc.) which may add up to a surprising total worth more than hurt pride?
4. What can I fall back on? (What are my current assets in the form of savings, bonds, insurance, etc.?)

An honest answer to these questions and others which are pertinent to your own personal needs can help you avoid the regrettable occurrence of becoming unemployed or settling for a job no better than the one you have.

The winds of reorganization always blow in a change of climate. How is the new temperature going to affect *you?* Even top heads roll before heavy gales!

Pete Gordon, former president of a midwest electrical company, found himself pushed down to middle management when his company encountered financial reverses. Hoping that Pete would somehow be reinstated to his former authority, his associates formed a loyal opposition to the new management. The battle lines grew and hardened to the point where both Pete and his successor had to look for new jobs. True to protocol, Pete had to go first—as the subordinate.

This was only the prelude to more management changes which eventually led to new ownership of the company and an almost complete overhaul of the executive personnel.

It was not the same in another company that also underwent the throes of reorganization:

Faced with a similar "loyal opposition" as confronted Pete Gordon's successor in the other company, the new president moved fast and forcefully to replace the loudest "rebel" among the old line supervisors.

Those remaining correctly read the handwriting on the wall and lost no time in buckling down to learning how to cooperate with the new ways. They are still there and prospering.

Play It Straight with Executive Know-How

The proper food for executive growth varies with each organizational environment. A large company poses more problems for the employee, but is the most fertile ground for executive development. Major corporations provide more complete interrelations, more room for specialization, greater diversity of supervisory needs, and more opportunity for advancement.

As previously noted, the peculiarly individual "mood" of each organization usually starts at the top, and that brings us to the rocky soil of office politics. Politicians naturally thrive in a climate where the top executives play politics, too. Where politicking is the way of life, it is not going to do you any good to merely "rise above" the "sordid" business by ignoring it. You have to know what is going on to protect yourself.

If you believe the "good guy" only wins in the Westerns, you are underestimating the powerful strategy of playing it straight. Playing it straight with executive know-how is about as "guileless" as the beautifully formed woman in the "plain little black dress"— one is no less devastating to the competition than the other!

In a large insurance company two executives had their sights on a "plum" that would be offered when one of the vice-presidents left the parent company to head up a subsidiary.

X was less qualified than Y, but this did not make him covet the position any less. If sheer determination and pulling of every available string could do it, X meant to wrest the job away from Y.

X left no stone unturned, leaving a trail of "whispering campaigns" and two-edged "compliments" like: "Y has enough to do. Let me handle that," and "That was a great snow job Y did on the Finance Committee; too bad he made old D. S. hot under the collar," and so on and on.

To his immense chagrin, X was making no progress with his campaign. Y was always one step ahead of him, and continued to distinguish himself quietly while effectively avoiding X's traps. When the final score was in, Y was fittingly the new vice-president. He had played it straight with executive know-how!

X lost not only because he was a little less qualified than Y, but also he had allowed his ambition to denigrate his associates and tried to hide his own limitations by talking down the abilities of others.

Now *you* play it straight but smart like this:

1. Watch the timing.
2. Learn what not to do.
3. Value your good name.

With executive know-how you can change your climate to better, but you have to:

Watch Your Timing!

Your boss's attitude toward you and your ideas often depends on whether he is tired, preoccupied, pleased, etc. To thrive, the subordinate must be quite certain to take his senior's attitude into account. The right timing can create rapport between you and your superiors. What may look like a good idea or improvement to you can be just one more pressure or headache for your boss if your timing is off.

Not only must management ask "How much is all this going to cost?" but also, "Do we have the proper facilities to put it across successfully?" There is the further question of "Has this or something like it already been tried and discarded?"

Your company is limited in the amount of expansion or innovation it can undertake at any one time. Remember that there is more at stake in acting on your proposal, than the satisfaction YOU may derive from seeing it become an action.

Know What Not To Do

Use your imagination and intelligence to project past experiences into the future. The ability to learn from past occurrences and to draw upon them in the future is why experienced men are at the top.

The school of hard knocks is not always the best place to learn, but it is the roughest. Make it easy on yourself—learn from other's mistakes.

An electrical engineer was regaling his associates with a recent ghastly experience. It seems that he had been selected to demonstrate before a large group of customers, his company's new, "unbreakable" tempered glass for watt-hour meters. You guessed it—the "unbreakable" glass shattered all over the stage and with it, said the young engineer, his nerves. "I had to be helped off the platform," he admitted.

It so happened that not long afterwards, one of his listeners was performing the same experiment, and with the same unfortunate result. Profiting from his colleague's earlier mishap, this young man rallied quickly and confided to his audience, "It will break once in a thousand times. I guess this was the thousandth." Whereupon he shrugged his shoulders and looked sorrowful while everybody enthusiastically applauded.

Executive know-how is also knowing what not to do as well as the desirable actions. The list of don'ts left in the wake of all the executive drop-outs would stretch from here to there, but a few pop up with enough consistency to serve as red flags.

Don't you wait to find out the hard way the wisdom of these critical don'ts:

1. *Don't* "upstage" your boss.
2. *Don't* jump the channels of communications.
3. *Don't* "step on" your subordinates.
4. *Don't* do too much too fast.

The smart executive aspirant knows that in any organization it pays to:

1. Make your boss look good.
2. Cooperate with the system.
3. Consider your subordinates.
4. Alternate your levels of achievement.

Make Your Boss Look Good

Sure, you want to look good, but to become the top man, become a "first-rate second man." It is one of those little human foibles that your worth in the eyes of your superior grows commensurately with how well you make him look. The best way to stop being a second man is to be a very good second man.

Brown's cost-cutting idea was not going over too well with his boss, B. J. Re-examination of the plan did not turn up any flaw. So why couldn't Brown put it across?

That night Brown took the outline home with him and once more pored over it. At last a flicker of understanding shone through. Why, this suggestion appeared to be critical of B. J.'s present method of operation. The entire presentation made his superior look remiss. No wonder he was giving it the cold shoulder.

Back to work went young Brown, and the next day he approached B. J. with his money saving idea wearing a new look. This time Brown praised the merits of the present system without at all detracting from the appeal of his own proposal. He and his boss both came out looking good.

Most of the time your boss is also an employee. Just like you he has a need to protect himself and his position. Don't make it impossible for him to act upon your suggestions without losing face or status.

Your boss has to justify his actions to his superior. He cannot always be as objective as you would wish. Like you, he sometimes has to choose the lesser of two evils. Like you, his status is always on the line and subject to being overruled by a higher authority. To get ahead—*work with him—and for him.*

In all discussions your boss has the floor. He can "ramble" if he chooses, but you must confine your role to listening, answering questions and offering comments, only when invited to do so. You are always on trial—your superiors are the judges.

Don't outdress your boss—let him look at least a little bit better. If you live in a small town or where such things are noticeable—let him drive the newest and most expensive car.

Nat Greene, President of the National Electric Coil Division of McGraw-Edison Company, did the next best thing. In his shiny new Cadillac, Nat drove out one day to pick up his boss, nationally known industrialist, Max McGraw. On the way back from the airport, Nat noticed Mr. McGraw fingering the elegant padded dashboard.

"What year Cadillac is this, Nat?" Mr. McGraw inquired. "The current model, Sir," admitted Nat proudly. "Oh, I drive a 1937 Pontiac myself," Mr. McGraw remarked.

As Nat later put it to me, "That was a real hot potato he handed me. Mr. McGraw could buy a railroad easier than I could purchase a ticket, but he chooses to drive his 'antique,' but moderately priced auto."

"What did you do?" I asked.

"I had to think fast," said Nat, "but I came up with, 'That's the best car General Motors ever made, and I can see why you are keeping it.' "

And said I, "It is easy to see why you are president of your company."

Cooperate with the System!

Communication channels are not all red tape; an orderly flow of communications promotes the maximum efficiency. To bypass or jump over the proper channels not only slows down the wheels of overall progress, it often slows *you* down in your climb up the executive ladder. I learned the hard way.

I once had a boss who always insisted everything go through his hands personally. He would never pass my "brain storms" up the ladder. It was an extremely trying time for one eager to make his mark.

I tried to get around him by button-holing the "big-boss" in the corridors, on the street, etc. I was too naive to realize that notwithstanding the merits of my ideas, the big man wasn't about to start implementing them over the head of my immediate superior. My "great ideas" died of old age, but I am grateful for the tolerance extended to me in this obnoxious period of self-development.

Don't tie up the channels by submitting irrelevant and unsolicited information to your superiors. Learn to distinguish between:

What you think he needs or should have.
What he needs.
What he specifies.

If you have a good idea or practical recommendation, state it discreetly and let your superior draw his own conclusions.

Don't make a pest of yourself when reasonable efforts to put across your ideas fail. Remember you do not "look good" if you appear to be personally turned down along with your offerings.

A history of rejections projects a "failure image" of you. When you approach your boss, try not to have him think, "Here he comes with another lame brain proposal," or when you leave, "I wonder what wild idea he'll come up with next."

So when you have an idea, think it through. Talk it over with your associates—don't be afraid someone will steal it. Chances are others wouldn't want to have it associated with them.

Any organizational climate is unhealthy for you if you insist on pinning your boss down or backing him into an untenable corner.

You Need Your Subordinates

Without subordinates you could hardly be called an executive. They can often make or break you. It's up to you. Run a "penny ante" shop and expect the quality of productivity to be correspondingly meager.

I know well the head and founder of a small manufacturing company in Chicago. This man is unusually well endowed with ability, determination and stick-to-itiveness. By most calculations, his company should be bigger and more prosperous. Why isn't it? Although he would be the last to recognize or admit it, his mistrust of subordinates is an albatross about his neck.

While visiting him one day, he interrupted our talk time after time to run out, first to check up on the two painters who might be "goofing off," then to peer over his secretary's shoulder to be sure that she was not using his time and materials to write personal letters, and once down to his little dungeon of a cellar to assure himself that some wasteful employee had not forgotten to turn off unneeded lights as he moved about. Consequently, all his workers dragged their feet like the slaves they were.

Certain actions beget predictable results, i.e., unfairness yields resentment, anger arouses more anger, fairness wins cooperation, etc.

The very young or "junior" executive frequently finds himself low-man on the totem pole of the management structure. The more personal benefits to be gained from placating your superiors naturally loom larger to you than "catering" to your subordinates, but play it straight with executive know-how. Earn your subordinates' respect and cooperation!

Create a Healthy Climate for Your Subordinates. It took Barry Auerbach only a few weeks to learn that at the Ace Van Lines, Inc., it was not what you knew that counted, but whom you knew. Most of the administrative staff had arrived at their present enviable positions with the ample assistance of influential backing. Overall, the executives were suitably (if not always outstandingly) qualified to perform their functions, but the general mood among the employees was one of dissatisfaction and resentment. The more ambitious workers toiled assiduously at "polishing the apple" as the only way to get ahead there.

Barry Auerbach did not see it that way; before long the word spread that Barry's subordinates were getting a "fair shake." G. R. Smith had just received a raise based on merit alone. Smith and Auerbach hardly spoke to each other except in the line of duty, but Auerbach had recognized and rewarded his subordinate for using his talent to get things done.

Did this change the climate at Ace Van Lines, Inc.? Yes, Barry's fair play tactics considerably improved the mood of his subordinates—for them the company had become a better place to work, and in time this gradually affected other departments. Today, if not exactly a democratic environment, the Ace Van Lines, Inc. boasts more opportunities for the rank and file workers, with a corresponding increase in job satisfaction, because one man played it straight!

A Smile Is Also Executive Know-How. A too formal senior-junior relationship puts undue pressure on your subordinates.

Your behavior is limited only by your own discretion, whereas your subordinate has to hold back his feelings.

Don't take out your own resentment toward your boss on your subordinates.

Don't Be Afraid of the "Comer." Learn to walk with him and you will both come out ahead. Rather than compete with him, hire another go-getter and let them compete with each other for your attention.

Playing it straight with executive know-how can pay off in unexpected ways. Mr. T. D. Barnes, Manager of Engineering, Meter Department of Westinghouse Electric Corporation, once had the experience of seeing his subordinate pass him on the way up to General Manager of the Measurements Division of his company. "At the time," says Mr. Barnes, "it was good to know that I always treated A. J. right when I was his boss."

Alternate Your Levels of Achievement

It Is Not Always the Climate That Holds You Back! Morris Reid was a very ambitious young man with all the necessary education and tested aptitudes when he started his career as the most junior executive of a large company. Not a bit afraid of hard work, Morris plunged in with zeal to make a name for himself.

Day in and day out, Morris extended himself to the utmost. Time after time he effectively put across good ideas. Management smiled on Morris. His supervisor patted him on the back; the words of encouragement were many—but that was all.

At that time there was nowhere for Morris (or his peers) to go in the organization; operations and personnel were frozen. Five or six years passed in this fashion before a door finally opened, but Morris did not go through it. Why not?

Reid's best had become commonplace; it now went unnoticed, and Morris was passed over by a relative newcomer whose fresher, more dramatic achievements were much more recently in the forefront.

Deeply wounded by this rejection, Morris left for greener pastures, where the whole dismal story was once more repeated, only this time Morris Reid was just that much older if not wiser.

It won't do you any good to migrate, unless you know why you have failed.

Reid fell into a trap all too common to strong, silent types who confuse playing it straight with playing it dumb. It is characteristic (and unfortunate) for such individuals to camouflage lofty aspirations behind a submissive exterior while relentlessly driving themselves to always achieve the spectacular.

Operating as loners, obediently they follow the party line, secretly hoping that superiors will reward them for their loyalty, efficiency, dedication, etc. Generally too timid to call attention to themselves in face-to-face confrontations with superiors, they try to do it by showing up their rivals, always hoping that those above them are mind readers who can recognize their dedication for what it often really is—consummate ambition.

Too much too fast deteriorates to ordinary for you. Don't consistently do such an outstanding job that your most is the least everybody expects from you. Play it straight with executive know-how like this:

Alternate the spectacular with the average. Strive to be just a little bit better than your major competition—with timely flashes of superior know-how.

Let us say that you have just put over a good idea; you are riding high. Enjoy it! Relax for a while—but not a long while. Give yourself and others a chance to digest this most recent "goody" before you come at them with another.

Here are four reasons why:

1. You need rest between major "dashes up the ladder."
2. The effect is more dramatic, and is more easily understood and appreciated when each achievement stands alone.
3. The quality does not keep up with the quantity.
4. You will "peak out." Others can't only think about your accomplishments, and jealousy will cause resentment and opposition.

Play your role straight but smart by being consistently above average. Excel in spurts—when you need attention drawn to your accomplishments. How can you be "just above average" and yet stand out for promotion? There is, of course, no one way to assure that you will be selected for advancement, but you must be willing to devote much effort toward self-improvement, including the building of goodwill with associates. All along the way, you thrive in terms of what you can get others to do, and how much you increase your company's worth.

VALUE YOUR GOOD NAME

An enviable reputation for integrity and straight shooting has a high price tag, but is worth every bit of it. Your growth potential in any organizational climate is going to be closely related to your reputation.

Young Malcolm was making great progress at the home office of a large New England based company, confides the Chairman of the Board. Malcolm had made the highest score ever recorded by an employee of that company on the aptitude tests conducted by a nationally known aptitude testing firm. In effect, it seemed that Malcolm had everything going for himself when he was given the keys to a new car in Hartford, Connecticut and a $500 travel advance to get him to the Cleveland, Ohio office.

It was late Friday afternoon when he departed with the best wishes of all his associates, but before Malcolm arrived in Cleveland on Tuesday, bills were being checked out by the Waldorf

Astoria Hotel, etc. The result was that Malcolm was welcomed with his discharge notice.

While many companies shy away from issuing specific instructions or guidance on expense accounts, the executives are expected to use prudent judgment. There are different reasons for absence of specific guidelines, the least delicate of which is to prevent the maximum expenses from becoming the minimum, thereby reducing all executives to the same level—unthinkable in the status structure of management.

Cast your most desirable image by always observing the following expense account principles:

1. *Keep accurate records of your expenses* with an explanation for any which are high or unusual.
2. *Treat company money as you would have others treat your own.* Aside from dishonesty, loose spending identifies the insecure, the unsophisticated and the show-off.
3. *Spend according to your position in the firm,* not necessarily in accordance with your personal resources.
4. *You only have to please the clients;* others need only be satisfied.

Learn to Use the Grapevine with Integrity

Every organization has a grapevine, but its information is not available to all. Indeed, you can work for years in a company and never be the recipient of a single "juicy" morsel of information! That is because it is very hard to be a recipient without also being a contributor.

So, if you are not a "talker," the chances are good that you will be excluded from much valuable knowledge as well as the inevitable idle gossip. How do you get on the inside without becoming a gossip or busybody? It takes executive know-how to be in on the grapevine without compromising yourself.

One way is to keep your ears open for "clean" items to feed the grapevine that do not downgrade, besmirch or ridicule others in the organization.

Let rumors stop with you. Courted by nosy workers and scheming superiors alike, the gossip is blindly lured into a trap of his own making. Observe the office gossip and notice how much time it takes to run an "information center"! See the years roll over these individuals as they operate at the same old non-profit, non-status stand.

The best way to be in the know is to be a good mixer. The lone hand does not thrive in the large organization climate. You don't have to be one of the boys every day, but you should sometimes accept invitations to lunch with your associates, enjoy occasional coffee breaks with them, and sometimes join them during off hours on golf courses, at bowling alleys, etc. Talking shop is a common part of off hours recreation, and any executive can tell you how much these free-time get togethers influence big decision making.

Getting nowhere with maneuvering and "diplomacy"? Try playing it completely straight—go directly to the principal and ask him outright for the desired information. You may be surprised at how many straightforward answers you get this "easy way." But be prepared to hear things you won't like.

When in turn, subordinates ask you questions that you are unprepared to answer, say honestly, "Sorry I cannot tell you that now."

"Do unto others as you would have them do unto you." It can be just that simple to play it straight with executive know-how!

Review

There are almost as many organizational climates as there are organizations.

Recognize the most favorable climate for *you*.

You thrive in any climate when you:

1. Complement your supervisor's needs better than anyone else.
2. Contribute to the company profits.
3. Make certain that your boss is always right. (If he has to lose for you to win, *you* are the bigger loser.)
4. Realize your boss is the most important (to you) person in the company.
5. Know the necessity of guarding against certain actions as well as the importance of doing others.
6. Span gaps with others by building bridges to them—not waiting for them to come to you.

7. Appreciate the value of the goodwill of others to advance and to stay on top.

8. Are aware that others need you only to the extent that you are willing to aid them in achieving their goals.

9. *Play it straight with executive know-how* like this·

   Talk less and *do* more.
   Be enthusiastic for the task at hand.
   Demonstrate superior ability to get things done.
   Value your reputation.
   Cultivate a sense of importance in the company, in yourself, and in others.

CHAPTER TEN

Turn Your Liabilities into Assets

The lives of great men all remind me that many success stories start out as tales of woe!

During the second World War the allied nations found their rubber supplies from foreign lands cut off. A serious rubber shortage developed that threatened the war effort. Out of that "handicap" came the magic product, synthetic rubber, which revolutionized the rubber industry and won lasting fame for Harvey Firestone, the genius behind the formula that launched the new and booming era of manmade fibers.

Einstein was a high school dropout—his inability to conform to the "average" was one of the clues to his later universally acclaimed genius.

Henry Ford never learned to write or speak fluently. He played hookey from school to "tinker" with water wheels and steam turbines. He was a total failure as a farm hand to his father—but he left that farm to become the century's foremost automotive engineer, a changer of history and the inventor of the world's best known automobile.

The first time that H. V. Kaltenborn tried to speak in public, he was a student at Harvard University. H. V.'s "debut" started out as a complete fiasco, as he often told later audiences. As soon as he opened his mouth on that memorable day a terrible thing happened—he completely forgot his carefully prepared speech! Then in desperation, that creative genius came to his aid, and the young

Kaltenborn told the story in his own words just as they came "off the top of his head." He won first prize and continued on to a fabulous career whose chief success ingredient was H.V.'s ability to speak spontaneously and eloquently "off the cuff."

Do you see the emergence of a "success pattern" in the backgrounds of these noted achievers? Together with countless others like them (famous and not famous), these men share at least one thing in common—the know-how to turn liabilities into assets.

"I would have accomplished less if I had lacked the prod of necessity," Harvey Firestone is quoted to have said after bringing his company out of one of its early setbacks. "Necessity forced upon me the need for low overhead. I had to be careful about the men I hired. Each employee was an investment." Because Harvey Firestone knew how to make wise use of all such "disadvantages," out of the "handicap" of small capital grew one of the financial empires of the world.

"If somebody hands you a lemon," Dale Carnegie used to say, "make a lemonade." I am all for that. Why screw up your face and try to suck a lemon when you can turn it into a refreshing drink? "Grin and bear it" has never been one of my pet philosophies, because it is so static. Living with your problems is not as bad as bowing under them, but you can do better than that:

In his teens, my good friend, Bill VanRavensway of the California Texas Oil Company, had a bone disease that impeded his ability to open his mouth very wide. He had difficulty even in eating, and it was very hard for Bill to put volume in his voice. Through intensive self-development, including speech therapy and public speaking, Bill is today an accomplished speaker. Only his dentist knows for sure that Bill has a speech impediment.

I doubt that anyone ever obtained more from the Dale Carnegie courses than Bill, probably due to the fact that no one could have prepared better for each session.

Not only the physically disabled are handicapped. We are all handicapped, one way or another, by personality flaws, bad habits, apathy, insufficient training, etc., *but* we are not handicapped by circumstances.

"I do not believe in circumstances," George Bernard Shaw once wrote. "The people who get on in this world are the ones who look for the circumstances they want, and if they can't find them, make them."

The varying qualities essential for executive performance lie primarily in those areas which can be influenced by your own actions. For example, you can control such factors as job knowledge, environment, work habits, interests, patriotism, self-control, attitudes and cooperation, consideration for the welfare of others, communicating ability, fairness, etc.

Mr. G. R. Weppler, President of Harvey Hubbell, Incorporated, puts that message to his executives this way: "No competitor can have a long-term advantage over us."

Make your own favorable circumstances by mastering the three "How's" of turning your liabilities into assets:

1. Think Positively.
2. Keep Going.
3. Make Your "Handicaps" Work *for* You.

Your ability to turn your liabilities into assets depends very much upon your attitude toward them.

THINK POSITIVELY

Your attitude makes the difference! Almost anything is a handicap if you think it is! A short time ago my attention was caught by this headline in the Sunday Supplement of the *Long Island Daily Press*: "Blind Teacher Doesn't Feel Handicapped"

It was the story of a teacher who discovered a few years ago that he was going blind. Today that professor and his seeing eye dog are a familiar and edifying sight on a Long Island high school campus. Everybody—parents, teachers, students—agree that the greatest beneficiaries of that man's positive thinking are the children who are learning "a little about life" along with the standard academic curriculum.

Most people think being fired is a big handicap in the race for executive success. When Ed Swanson's employment with a large airplane manufacturer on Long Island was terminated after fifteen years, he was depressed and looked around for another field of endeavor. My good friend Truman Weller, then Manager of the Northeastern Section of the Chamber of Commerce of the United States, prevailed on Ed to remain in his chosen field.

"The door of opportunity opened to me," said Ed who used the "unfortunate" occasion to move on to a much more prominent position at several thousand dollars more compensation with an airplane manufacturer on the West Coast.

Your personality is the manifestation of your individual attitudes and traits. They follow an organized pattern, creating your individual character. Very often people are unaware of their attitudes and overlook the significance of this aspect of their make-up.

An important attitude is how you feel about your chosen work. Do you like it and do you perform outstandingly? If the answer is "no," it does not always mean lack of executive ability. Very often a change in your attitude can make the vital difference!

Perhaps right now you are chafing in your role of follower. You itch to get your hands on the reins; you feel "handicapped" because you have to wait. Look at it this way:

Business Leaders Never Stop Being Followers. There is always the board of directors, the stockholders, clients, government, etc. Therefore, playing well the follower role is an *asset* to the would-be executive.

Indeed, so important is the preliminary training as a follower that management courses now feature special instruction in followership—for the new college graduate or junior executive who has been "handicapped" by not working his way up through the lower ranks.

The best followers become the best leaders. But, should you become trapped in the role of a lowlier follower than that to which you aspire, don't look upon it as a tragic handicap. It could be your most profitable role, if it is what you do best! A good second man is worth his weight in gold to the busy executive:

Two young men started up the executive ladder in the same company. A was the owner's son. This "asset" assured him his future, therefore A could take it easy. He did not have to cultivate friends in the industry or "try" for promotions.

On the other hand, B had to fight the "liability" of competing with the boss's son. There was only one way for B to keep up with A; B had to develop more executive know-how. This he did, by directing all his innate ability toward self-improvement and performance. B made friends and influenced others to the extent that today, although A is in charge, B is the key man in keeping the organization going.

"In a world crammed with leaders it is easy to see that the

follower's role is unlimited." (From *Executive's Digest*, April, 1968.)

Don't Worry

For many, worry is the major handicap. Worry puts a great strain on the nervous system often resulting in various forms of physical and mental disorders. The price of worrying is too high to pay. Too often worry is a fear of intangibles or events that will never happen. I know a prosperous dentist who worries about having nothing to worry about!

What do you do when you have given your all and do not make the grade? Will you allow failure to gnaw away at you, or will you throw in the towel immediately, and rush off to try your luck in a new arena? You can fall back on wishful thinking, become a griper who makes work harder for the others, die a little more each day, but none of these tactics will help you to find out *why* you failed.

When William P. Kirkwood was a young man and passed over in an organizational shake-up, he wasted no time in self-pity. Instead, Bill decided to improve his executive know-how, and promptly set about that task with enthusiastic determination.

How did his positive attitude pay off? Today Bill is the president of that company which now bears his name, and he is also the head of a second company!

Try my mother-in-law's effective therapy for job anxiety. Imagine the worst that can happen, and then think about what you could do in that eventuality. Resolve not to dissipate your energies opposing things over which you have no control or influence. Think of your troubles as day-by-day events, not as life sentences. Use your best judgment to control those factors over which you have dominion.

To think positively, review your past performance not only in terms of achievement, but in the areas of your personal liabilities and human relations. Professional help is available in appraising aptitudes (achievement, intelligence and psychological tests), as well as in career counseling, if you honestly wish to evaluate what went wrong. Take the best course for *you*.

The first step toward developing a positive attitude is to have a sincere desire to improve your possible performance by reducing your personal limitations (liabilities). Second, you must determine just what your limitations are, because realistic goals can be established only in light of what you can do to modify those characteristics which can prevent the accomplishment of desired objectives.

The foregoing can get you through the working part of the day, but what about after working hours? Use these times to relax and get the peace of mind and the rest you need, or your nerves will eventually get the best of your self-control.

When you leave your place of work, think only positive thoughts. Don't carry grudges, and forget about "paying back in kind" when someone hurts you. Grievances and offenses (real or imaginary) are best forgotten as soon as possible. Don't expect others to be always grateful for favors you have rendered; you forget sometimes too!

The best way to cure worry is to prevent it. You will be less prone to worry when you are physically fit. Good health requires adequate food, exercise, relaxation and rest. The last is extremely important, so that your body can rebuild itself. An executive's day is a full one. Plan for mental breaks during the course of each day.

An organized approach to your work can materially reduce the frustration factor. Keep on your desk only what is relevant to the task at hand. Establish a priority system (most important things first). Once you have made a decision, let it stand; don't vacillate or second guess yourself. Take care of problems as they come up, and avoid procrastination. Problems have a way of building up alarmingly.

Slice away great chunks of anxiety with these five worry chasers:

1. Accept criticism without displaying rancor.
2. Tackle problems in the order of their importance.
3. Render satisfactory decisions.
4. Discuss debatable topics in a dispassionate manner aimed at arriving at the truth.
5. Count your blessings!

Item number 5 may sound old-fashioned, but it is hard to improve on the old maxims which have been tried in the furnace of experience and found valid. When you are feeling sorry for yourself, think of the beggar who was sad because he had no shoes, until he met the beggar who had no feet.

Throw off those disturbing thoughts, and plunge into your work with abandonment. Determine not to fret over inconsequential matters, and:

KEEP GOING

The ability to turn handicaps and setbacks into assets depends very much upon your ability to keep going though handicapped.

After many years of traveling for the midwestern branch of the Fleetwood Steel Plate Company as their Sales Manager, Mr. F. G. Elliott suffered a mild heart attack that make it unwise for him to continue traveling. Since this had been the essence of Mr. Elliott's responsibility for so long, he did not know in which direction to go from there.

But Elliott did not stop—he kept going. Just when things seemed hopeless, he found an excellent job for a man with his sales background and no traveling!

A vice-president of a major manufacturing company in Connecticut contracted polio after he was married. Thinking he was all washed up as a useful member of society, he stopped fighting and resigned himself to the life of a helpless cripple. To get him going again, his doctor recommended a shock treatment. Accordingly his wife would take her husband protestingly to the swimming pool and throw the "helpless cripple" in, saying, "Swim or drown, the choice is yours!"

He swam, as the doctors felt he would. He is still going strong as an executive, is a state champion square dance caller, and you must look carefully to even note the slighest limp in his walk.

In my own case, I was forced to take a medical discharge from the Army during the height of the second World War. They told me to go home and enjoy my family as much as I could until I died—very soon was the obvious inference. I returned home, taught high school math and marching; then did my bit for defense as a mechanics instructor, went back to college, started out in my profession, completed graduate work at Columbia University, and here I am, the father of six children, earning my keep, and still going.

From his wheelchair, Franklin Delano Roosevelt guided the United States through more than a decade of its most turbulent years. Roosevelt's crippling illness set limits upon his physical mobility, but the wheelchair was never able to restrain the man's great spirit, which kept going at an enthusiastic pace.

Through his inspiration, the pain and suffering of thousands of physically disabled were relieved and aided in living normal lives. The March of Dimes Foundation, created to defeat a dreaded crippler of children, succeeded in its goal, and people all over the world are the direct beneficiaries.

Defeatism is a negative attitude that declares the battle is lost before even the first shot is fired. It is the opposite of courage and enthusiasm. Fight this handicap with huge doses of courage and enthusiasm for the job at hand. Strike "can't" and "impossible" from your vocabulary and keep going.

Make Your Handicaps Work for You

Irving Mande, Chief Engineer of Edwards Company, Inc. is a "pro" at turning liabilities into assets. At times this meant giving his executive know-how a real workout:

A few years ago, Irving had to share a secretary with other executives—a big handicap for all of them. In the midst of this uncomfortable situation the management sought to increase Irving's scope of responsibility.

Although flattered and eager for the added assignment, Irving did not jump right on the opportunity. After a couple of days of reflection, he announced his decision. Yes, he would be most happy to handle the additional work, but to do it right without diminishing his effectiveness in his present duties, Irving would need additional secretarial assistance. He got his private secretary.

Irving knew that the best time to obtain concessions from others is when they are seeking to motivate you. In this case, management obtained what it wanted, and Irving felt that he could do a more effective job for his company.

Daniel Woodhead, Jr. and James A. Edmonds are Chairman and President, respectively of the Daniel Woodhead Company. They started about the same time with the company, but Dan was the son of the founder of the firm.

Dan says he was a "terrible salesman"; whereas Jim excelled in that area. Consequently, Dan turned his efforts to the financial end of the business, and became an expert in that area. This limited his outside contacts with clients.

Jim, on the other hand, built up friends for his company as he endeavored to make sales. Together they make a formidable team with each recognizing the major contributions of the other.

Dan concentrated his efforts in an area which was compatible with his personality, and Jim made a major role for himself by filling the "void" of the owner's son.

Put your handicaps to work *for* you by doing "what comes naturally."

Bob Hope, Jimmy Durante, and Danny Thomas are all estimable entertainers. Certainly, none of them would ever win a male beauty contest—their famous long noses would get in the way. But just see the mileage they have all gotten out of that "handicap." Look at the midget who is just right for those tight work spaces—such as a riveter in the tail section of an airplane, etc.

I have heard that the late Walt Disney's friends once warned him that, "You can't make money in show business without 'blue' stories." But Disney chose to cling to his natural predilection for clean family entertainment, and you know how that worked for him.

Take that old cliché: "Those who can't, teach." Many fine teachers are aroused to resentful defensiveness by that sentiment, but they need not be. Its stigma rubs off with a little insight into the words, "can't" and "teach." The fact that a scientist fails to come up with a world-shaking discovery and goes on to turn out scientists who do make those spectacular breakthroughs, means only one thing: He is a gifted teacher, not just another average scientist.

If you can communicate your know-how to others better than you can do it yourself, that communicating ability is your real talent. Recognize it for what it is and be proud of it! The field of education then becomes *your* arena of success.

Not long ago a famous illustrator (who doesn't care to publicize his experience) was fired from an advertising agency because he had "no talent for the work." Whereupon the artist took his "no talent" to a sophisticated metropolitan magazine, which welcomed him with open arms and ushered him into the heady world of fame and fortune.

Take a good look at your personal "liabilities." Are some of them perhaps disguised *assets*?

I knew the manager of a large department store chain who was terribly self-conscious about his "John L. Lewis type of eyebrows." He had tried many times, with poor results, to trim the offending hairs into a more pleasing shape. So my friend went about in a generally unhappy state, until one day he overheard the following conversation between two of his more promising subordinates:

"The other day at the sales conference, I almost put my foot in my mouth, until I saw old —— (the Manager) looking daggers at me. With those eyes and that hairy frown, he can freeze you in your tracks. The old boy can keep you in line without ever opening his mouth. All he has to do is to look at you. Brr!"

From then on, the "old boy" stopped interfering with nature and now immensely enjoys his liability turned asset. The last time I saw him, he gleefully confided that his wife now thought of his eyebrows as "sexy."

Below is a list of personal handicaps to which most of us are prone. Can you separate the "dyed in the wool" liabilities from those, that with a little proper treatment, are hidden assets?

Aloofness	Inarticulation
Bias (Prejudice)	Indecision
Carelessness (Indifference)	Inertia
Conceit (Subjectiveness)	Inferiority Complex
Dependence	Inflexibility
Defeatism (Quitter)	Instability
Dullness	Insincerity
Evasiveness	Insensitiveness
Excessiveness	Irresponsibility
Fear	Procrastination
Forgetfulness	Selfishness
Immaturity	Shyness
Impatience	Slovenliness
Impulsiveness	Unreliability
Inability	Unsociability

Take a Good Look at:

Aloofness	Forgetfulness
Conceit	Impatience
Dependence	Impulsiveness
Evasiveness	Procrastination
Fear	Shyness

Aloofness can become an *asset,* if it means withdrawal from petty gossip, false rumors and "politicking." It is a handicap when it means non-involvement with your fellow beings—manifested by coolness and indifference to the plight of others. People are instinctively put on the defensive by the aloof individual, thereby suffering a loss of pride and enthusiasm in their efforts.

Conceit can be toned down into the *asset* of self-confidence. Conceit differs from self-confidence in that the latter implies recognition of one's real ability to perform, and the other is an expression of self-love—seldom justified. Conceit, whether founded upon real or imagined talent, will arouse resentment and prejudice.

Dependence is not too far away from becoming the *asset* of cooperation, in which you recognize your need to help others and to let them help you. Excessive dependence upon others for moral support or responsibility is definitely not an executive trait. Naturally, we cannot all be leaders, but those who guide and direct others must be imbued with a large share of dependability. To overcome the handicap of overdependence, you must begin by willingly accepting responsibility for your own actions.

Evasiveness can be an *asset.* To the uninitiated there appears little distinction between evasiveness and deceitfulness, but there is a difference. Deceitfulness is simply untruthfulness, whereas evasiveness is avoidance of being specific—allowing others to form their own mental image.

For example, if you falsify a report, you would be deceitful and consequently dishonest. Dishonesty can never be anything but a handicap; however, evasiveness, skillfully applied, can be executive know-how that gets you out of a "tight spot" when you need more time to explore all the angles before committing yourself.

Fear is an *asset* when it makes you realistically cautious about approaching areas of real danger. The control of fear requires the experiencing of success where you expected failure; it is mostly a state of mind between the limits of caution and cowardliness. For the executive, inordinate apprehension is a serious liability in the areas of responsibility and decision making where courage is essential.

Forgetfulness is also executive know-how when you are smart enough to forget imagined wrongs, unavoidable mistakes (yours as well as others), and to let bygones be bygones.

The mental liability of forgetfulness is more easily overcome than many others. There are many books and articles giving simple exercises and practical hints in memory training that are extremely effective, if diligently applied over a period of time. The ability to remember is an important executive attribute which can be developed if you are willing to make the personal effort to do so.

Impulsiveness can be an *asset*—spontaneous generosity, sympathy, praise, etc. Unfortunately, the executive whose actions are mostly triggered by emotional or involuntary impulses will find it hard to command the proper respect for his position. By their very nature, impulsive actions are seldom the most judicious.

Impulsiveness is a decided handicap when judgment does not consist of reflection and consideration of the relevant factors.

Impatience can be an *asset*. While not a totally destructive trait in an executive, it may be a hindrance to the establishment of mutual rapport. Subordinates are usually less motivated than their leaders, and they must be allowed time to perform without your breathing down their backs as they work.

If your impatience takes the form of leading others effectively to achieve change, to overcome those factors hindering the attainment of the objectives of the work unit, it is a definite executive attribute. You should, however, restrain strong urges for the sake of long-term success in the human relations area.

Procrastination can be executive know-how when it means deferring action to get the whole view, or until you can review the facts; this is not the same thing as delaying because you are reluctant to face up to the responsibility of reaching and implementing a decision.

On the other hand, constantly putting off until tomorrow what should be done today can become an ingrained trait—difficult to correct. There is also the possibility that one of those tomorrows you will be too old to take advantage of the opportunities available to you today.

Shyness can be an *asset*. A little natural reticence or modesty is a becoming trait, but excessive shyness or bashfulness that causes you to shrink from close contact with others is a handicap.

If you are too shy, force yourself to speak up with simple assurance every time you have a worthwhile suggestion to make. Join clubs, make friends, and find new interests, as antidotes for shyness which is merely a form of self-absorption.

See what the right treatment can do for many of your "faults."

Selfishness and anger have a bad reputation, but that is because of a narrow conception of what they really are! Take selfishness, for example: "The human race has endured through the ages on the concept of the survival of the fittest—the very epitome of selfishness. The greatest heights we attain as humans—patriotism, parenthood and friendship are all based on this same human trait—selfishness." (From J. F. Lincoln, *Intelligent Selfishness and Manufacturing*, Cleveland, Ohio: Lincoln Electric Company, 1943)

The word "intelligent" is the clue to turning many personal liabilities into assets. Exploiting your subordinates is selfish but not intelligent, therefore your selfishness becomes a very real handicap to your executive progress.

> You want to get ahead—that's selfish.
> Your subordinates want security—that's selfish.
> Your company wants to make a profit—that's selfish.
> *All* of you help each other to achieve your individual objectives—that's selfishness, but an *asset* to all of you.

You can apply this same "treatment" to anger—another much maligned, but human trait. Emotional control is exactly what it says—the control of one's emotions; it does not mean the absence of emotions. Passion for a cause or belief in your own capabilities is very much a leadership attribute. Enthusiasm, for example, is a passionate emotion. There is such a thing as "analyzing" all your emotions to the point of absolute sterility. Down through the ages many people had to be terribly angry or terribly glad to bring about what we call progress.

The late Reverend Martin Luther King, Jr. scaled the heights of inspired leadership, because he was an *angry* man—angry at social injustice. And let us not forget that classic example of all righteous anger—Jesus, with fire in his eyes and upraised arm, driving the money lenders out of the sacred temple.

The secret of successful emotional self-indulgence is intelligent control.

Be angry or glad to a purpose. Both anger and joy are liabilities or assets, depending on what you do under the influence of either. If your subordinate's inefficiency drives you to berate and shame him, your behavior is a handicap to your executive development.

Make your anger work for you by directing it at your lack of executive know-how to elicit the desired performance. Get out your executive tools, and see which ones you need for that particular job.

Intelligent control is also necessarily applicable to your virtues. While virtue may be its own reward, you can have too much of a good thing! In that case your asset becomes a liability. I once worked with a cocky young engineer who constantly boasted to one and all that he never read "anything but scientific and technical material." That was the dullest fellow I ever knew; what a bore he was.

Examine the moral, mental and physical characteristics of executive practices as a means of detecting that behavior which springs from emotions or other biological factors. Your body is the most complex mechanism known; yet you can direct it to achieve your desired goals.

By studying the underlying causes of your emotions, you can reduce their adverse impact on others and eliminate visible anxieties.

Successful executive know-how calls for your insight into the attitudes and behavior of others. To understand the actions of others, first note how you affect them, then try to correct those elements that restrain your effectiveness. Most difficulties in human relations are caused by *controllable* personality traits.

No matter how well endowed you are with plus factors, any significant liability can nullify them. The most frequent stopper of the ambitious executive is his superior's verdict: "He is so outstanding for . . . , but he worries me with his lack of tact . . . (or other objectional trait)." That "but" is often the reason why a promotion or raise goes to another.

If you think of success strictly in terms of self-aggrandizement and increased personal wealth, you are starting out "handicapped." Over and over again, lasting success has been founded upon service to others. Look at all the great tycoons, past and present—Andrew Carnegie, Rockefeller, Henry Ford, Eli Whitney, James Fulton, Sears & Roebuck, Montgomery Ward and George Westinghouse— to mention but a few. They, and many more, became great as a result of serving the public. You can change a naturally selfish desire to get ahead into an asset, simply by directing it toward helping others (your company, its clients and your co-workers) achieve their goals.

Review

Do not bemoan your "fate." An objective look will show that many of your handicaps relate to shortcomings in your own personality and limitations on your capabilities which you can directly control.

To turn your liabilities into assets you need to think positively.

You can alter or at least neutralize the objectional attitudes of others (handicaps to your executive development) by orientation, instead of aggravating these liabilities with nagging or fault finding.

Since attitudes are emotional in nature, you can do something about your own or those of others—once they have been identified.

Review your own performance, not only in terms of achievement, but also in the areas of personal liabilities and human relations.

Keep going. Don't let worry handicap you to the extent that you become subjective and fret constantly over your own fears.

Learn to distinguish accurately between true liabilities and hidden assets. Many traits are either liabilities or assets, depending on how you use them.

"To thine own self be true." Some of your "handicaps" may be clues to the real *you*. Doing what comes naturally can pay off— when you know *who* you really are.